QUALITATIVE AND QUANTITATIVE METHODS
IN EVALUATION RESEARCH

Volume 1
SAGE RESEARCH PROGRESS SERIES IN EVALUATION

SAGE RESEARCH PROGRESS SERIES IN EVALUATION

General Editor: SUSAN E. SALASIN, *National Institute of Mental Health*
Co-Editor (1979): ROBERT PERLOFF, *University of Pittsburgh*

EDITORIAL REVIEW BOARD

SAGE RESEARCH PROGRESS SERIES IN EVALUATION
Volume 1

Edited by
THOMAS D. COOK
and
CHARLES S. REICHARDT

QUALITATIVE AND QUANTITATIVE METHODS IN EVALUATION RESEARCH

Published in cooperation with the
EVALUATION RESEARCH SOCIETY

 **SAGE** PUBLICATIONS Beverly Hills   London

For information address:

SAGE Publications, Inc.
275 South Beverly Drive
Beverly Hills, California 90212

SAGE Publications Ltd
28 Banner Street
London EC1Y 8QE, England

Printed in the United States of America

Library of Congress Cataloging in Publication Data
Main entry under title:

Qualitative and quantitative methods in evaluation research.

   (Sage research progress series in evaluation; v. 1)
   "Papers delivered at the 2nd annual meeting of the Evaluation Research Society held in Washington, DC. on November 2-31, 1978."
   Bibliography: p.
   1. Social sciences—Methodology—Congresses. 2. Evaluation research (Social action programs)—Congresses. I. Cook, Thomas D. II. Reichardt, Charles S. III. Evaluation Research Society. IV. Series.
H62.A1034   300'.7'23   79-20962
ISBN 0-8039-1300-1
ISBN 0-8039-1301-X pbk.

SECOND PRINTING

Photographic Credits

The two photographs by Bill Owens originally appeared in his book, *Suburbia,* San Francisco: Straight Arrow Books, 1973, and are reprinted with his permission. *Suburbia* is now available for $7.95 (plus $1.00 postage) from the author, Bill Owens, Box 687, Livermore, CA 94550.

The two photographs from Michael Lesy's book *Real Life: Louisville in the Twenties,* New York: Pantheon, 1976, are reprinted courtesy of the Photographic Archives, University of Louisville, Louisville, Kentucky 40208.

The photograph by Howard S. Becker is reprinted with his permission.

The photograph of the Entwistle family is from *City Families: Chicago and London* by Roslyn Banish. Copyright © 1974, 1975 by Roslyn Banish. Reprinted with permission of Pantheon Books, a division of Random House, Inc.

The photograph of Walker Evans is from the Farm Security Administration Collection, courtesy of the Library of Congress Photoduplication Service.

Contents

ABOUT THIS SERIES

The SAGE RESEARCH PROGRESS SERIES IN EVALUATION is a series of concisely edited works designed to present notable, previously unpublished writing on topics of current concern to the evaluation community. In keeping with a vision of evaluation as a methodological enterprise with outcomes at both the policy-making and services delivery levels, the series is designed to present state-of-the-art volumes for use by instructors and students of evaluation, researchers, practitioners, policy-makers, and program administrators.

Each volume (4 to 6 new titles will be published in each calendar year) focuses on themes which emerge from the previous year's annual meeting of the Evaluation Research Society—revised and supplemented by specially commissioned works.

The series begins in 1979 with five volumes, largely selected from papers delivered at the 2nd Annual Meeting of the Evaluation Research Society held in Washington, D.C. on November 2-4, 1978. The volumes in this inaugural year include:

*QUALITATIVE AND QUANTITATIVE METHODS IN EVALUATION RESEARCH, edited by Thomas D. Cook and Charles S. Reichardt

*EVALUATOR INTERVENTIONS: Pros and Cons, edited by Robert Perloff

*TRANSLATING EVALUATION INTO POLICY, edited by Robert F. Rich

*THE EVALUATOR AND MANAGEMENT, edited by Herbert C. Schulberg and Jeanette M. Jerrell

*EVALUATION IN LEGISLATION, edited by Franklin M. Zweig

We are pleased that these initial volumes in the *SAGE RESEARCH PROGRESS SERIES IN EVALUATION* so well represent significant interdisciplinary contributions to the literature. Comments and suggestions from our readers will be welcomed.

SERIES EDITORS:

Susan E. Salasin, National Institute of Mental Health
Robert Perloff, University of Pittsburgh

Charles S. Reichardt

University of Denver

Thomas D. Cook

Northwestern University

1

BEYOND QUALITATIVE *VERSUS* QUANTITATIVE METHODS

Considerable disagreement exists over the appropriateness of various methods and methodological stances for conducting evaluation research. One debate of growing intensity centers on the distinction between quantitative and qualitative methods. By quantitative methods, researchers have come to mean the techniques of randomized experiments, quasi-experiments, paper and pencil "objective" tests, multivariate statistical analyses, sample surveys, and the like. In contrast, qualitative methods include ethnography, case studies, in-depth interviews, and participant observation. Each of these method-types—i.e., quantitative and qualitative—has acquired a separate constituency of advocates who argue that it is their preferred methods which are best suited to evaluation. Below is a sample of the opinions supporting each side of this debate.

Campbell and Stanley (1966) and Riecken et al. (1974) are often cited as staunch proponents of quantitative methods. Although Campbell and Stanley (1966: 2) were not primarily concerned with evaluation research, they describe the experiment as "the only way of establishing a cumulative tradition in which improvements can be introduced without the danger of a faddish discard of old wisdom in favor of inferior novelties." Riecken et al. (1974: 6, 12) are only slightly more moderate in their claims about experiments and no less enthusiastic: "Experiments not only lead to clearer

AUTHORS' NOTE: *Work on this chapter was partially supported by a Faculty Research Grant of the University of Denver, a Faculty Research Grant from the W. T. Grant Foundation, and National Science Foundation Grant DAR78-09368. The authors thank Barbara Minton and Dale Schellenger for their helpful comments on earlier drafts of the manuscript.*

7

causal inferences, but the very process of experimental design helps to clarify the nature of the social problem being studied." "When conditions are not problematic or when the creativity and ingenuity of the research designer can resolve difficult problems, then experimentation is the *method of choice* for obtaining reliable and valid information upon which to plan social programs" (emphasis in the original).

Among others, Weiss and Rein (1972), Parlett and Hamilton (1976), and Guba (1978) are on the side of the debate supporting qualitative methods. In particular, Weiss and Rein (1972: 243) suggest several alternative research strategies deriving from the qualitative tradition which they believe "in general to be superior to experimental design as a methodology for evaluating broad-aim programs." In speaking specifically of educational evaluation, Parlett and Hamilton (1976: 141) quite forcefully add:

> Characteristically, conventional approaches have followed the experimental and psychometric traditions dominant in educational research. Their aim (unfulfilled) of achieving fully "objective methods" has led to studies that are artificial and restricted in scope. We argue that such evaluations are inadequate for elucidating the complex problem areas they confront and, as a result, provide little effective input to the decision-making process. . . . Illuminative evaluation is introduced as belonging to a contrasting "anthropological research paradigm."

Similarly, Guba (1978: 81) argues that naturalistic inquiry (which is likened to ethnographic fieldwork and investigative journalism, and is presented as being diametrically opposed to conventional, experimental inquiry) offers "a more congenial and responsive mode of evaluation than any other practiced today."

Current thinking is actually in more disagreement than indicated by these two sets of quotes. There is, indeed, a disagreement over whether or not there is a disagreement. For example, Rossi and Wright (1977: 13) claim that "there is almost universal agreement among evaluation researchers that the randomized controlled experiment is the ideal model for evaluating the effectiveness of public policy." Guba (1978) cites this statement with obvious disdain.

The purpose of the present chapter is to suggest that part of this current debate over qualitative and quantitative methods is not centered on productive issues and so is not being argued in as logical a fashion as it should be. This is not to suggest that a complete resolution of this methodological dispute is possible. As later discussed, there are important questions arising from the debate which allow honest differences of opinion and judgment. It would be fully appropriate for expression of sentiments, such as contained in at least some of the above quotes, to continue to be elaborated. But the debate, as it is coming more and more to be carried out, is obscuring issues and unnecessarily creating schisms between the two method-types, when it should be building bridges and clarifying the genuine disagreements that deserve attention.

THE LANGUAGE OF THE CURRENT DEBATE

To understand some of the fallacies in current thinking that are becoming popular, one must come to appreciate more fully how the debate between method-types is being waged. Recent commentators, critics, and advocates (cf. Guba, 1978; Parlett and Hamilton, 1976; Patton, 1975, 1978; Rist, 1977; and Wilson, 1977) view the debate not merely as a disagreement over the relative advantages and disadvantages of qualitative and quantitative methods but as a fundamental clash between methodological paradigms. According to this view, each method-type is associated with a separate and unique paradigmatic perspective and it is these two perspectives which are in conflict. As Rist (1977: 43) states the case, "Ultimately, the issue is not research strategies, *per se*. Rather, the adherence to one paradigm as opposed to another predisposes one to view the world and the events within it in profoundly differing ways."

The concept of paradigm is borrowed from Kuhn (1962, 1970). Building upon that work, Patton (1978: 203) defines a paradigm as

> a world view, a general perspective, a way of breaking down the complexity of the real world. As such, paradigms are deeply embedded in the socialization of adherents and practitioners: paradigms tell them what is important, legitimate, and reasonable. Paradigms are also normative, telling the practitioner what to do without the necessity of long existential or epistemological consideration.

Those who see the debate in terms of a contrast between paradigms usually provide a shopping list of attributes which are said to distinguish the qualitative and quantitative world views. For example, Rist (1977) offers three attributes, Patton (1978) provides seven, and Guba (1978) gives fourteen. Without attempting to be exhaustive, many of the prominent attributes of each paradigm are presented in Table 1. In brief, the quantitative paradigm is said to have a positivistic, hypothetico-deductive, particularistic, objective, outcome-oriented, and natural science world view. In contrast, the qualitative paradigm is said to subscribe to a phenomenological, inductive, holistic, subjective, process-oriented, and

Table 1: Attributes of the Qualitative and Quantitative Paradigms

Qualitative Paradigm	Quantitative Paradigm
Advocates the use of qualitative methods.	Advocates the use of quantitative methods.
Phenomonologism and verstehen; "concerned with *understanding* human behavior from the actor's own frame of reference."[a]	Logical-positivism; "seeks the *facts* or *causes* of social phenomena with little regard for the subjective states of individuals."[a]
Naturalistic and uncontrolled observation.	Obtrusive and controlled measurement.
Subjective.	Objective.
Close to the data; the "insider" perspective.	Removed from the data; the "outsider" perspective.
Grounded, discovery-oriented, exploratory, expansionist, descriptive, and inductive.	Ungrounded, verification-oriented, confirmatory, reductionist, inferential, and hypothetico-deductive.
Process-oriented.	Outcome-oriented.
Valid; "real," "rich," and "deep" data.	Reliable; "hard," and replicable data.
Ungeneralizable; single case studies.	Generalizable; multiple case studies.
Holistic.	Particularistic.
Assumes a dynamic reality.	Assumes a stable reality.

a. Quotes from Bogdan and Taylor (1975: 2). We would not necessarily subscribe to these descriptions of "phenomenologism" and "logical-positivism" (cf., Cook and Campbell, 1979), though such characterizations are widespread.

social anthropological world view. Filstead's discussion of the paradigms (this volume) provides a much more thorough and detailed description.

Such paradigmatic characterizations are based on two assumptions which are of direct consequence to the debate over methods. First, it is assumed that a method-type is irrevocably linked to a paradigm so that an allegiance to a paradigm provides the appropriate and sole means of choosing between method-types. That is, because they see the world in different ways, researchers must use different methods of inquiry. If one's theory of evaluation is more closely related to the attributes of paradigm A than to the attributes of paradigm B, one should automatically favor those research methods that are linked to paradigm A. Second, the qualitative and quantitative paradigms are assumed to be rigid and fixed, and the choice between them is assumed to be the only choice available. That is, the paradigms are considered to be cast in stone so that modifications, or other options, are not possible.

Intentionally or not (and in some discussions the intent is clearly not present), these two assumptions ultimately lead to the conclusion that qualitative and quantitative methods themselves can never be used together. Since the methods are linked to different paradigms and since one must choose between these mutually exclusive and antagonistic world views, one must also choose *between* the method-types.

Treating the method-types as incompatible obviously encourages researchers to use only one or the other when it may be a combination of the two that is best suited to research needs. It also paralyzes any attempt at reconciling the differences between the opposing sides of the debate over method-types. For these reasons, the conceptualization of the method-types as antagonistic may well be leading astray current methodological debate and practice. It is our view that the paradigmatic perspective which promotes this incompatibility between the method-types is in error. Specifically, both of the above assumptions are incorrect, so the conclusion, that researchers must choose between the method-types, does not hold. In the discussion below, we demonstrate the fallacy of both of these assumptions (i.e., the linkage between *paradigm* and *method*, and the forced choice between qualitative and quantitative paradigms). Having thus reconsidered the conflict between paradigmatic viewpoints, we then redefine the issues raised by the debate over method-types and highlight some of the potential benefits of using qualitative and quantitative methods *together*.

DO PARADIGMS LOGICALLY DETERMINE
THE CHOICE OF RESEARCH METHOD?

According to current usage, a paradigm includes not only a philosophical world view but also a linkage to a certain type of research method. In this definitional sense, then, a paradigm does determine the method. The question asked here is whether this linkage between paradigm and method is necessary and inherent or merely one of definition and practice. In other words, is there an inherent inconsistency in subscribing to the philosophy of one paradigm but employing the methods of the other? The question is easily answered by considering each of the paradigmatic attributes in turn to see if it is logically linked to only one of the methods or if it can apply equally well to both. Each attribute in Table 1 is discussed separately below.

Reconsidering the Linkage Between Paradigm and Method

• Is the researcher who uses quantitative procedures necessarily a logical positivist, and conversely, is the researcher who uses qualitative procedures necessarily a phenomenologist? Certainly not, for, on the one hand, many social researchers who use quantitative methods subscribe to a phenomenological stance. For example, social psychological theories of attribution are phenomenological in that they are aimed at understanding behaviors and beliefs from the perspective of the actors themselves. Yet most, if not all, of attribution research is conducted in the laboratory with quantitative methods. Or consider research on introspection, a topic which is again clearly in the realm of phenomenologism. In Nisbett and Wilson's (1977) review of research on introspection, the vast majority of studies used quantitative procedures such as the randomized experiment and "objective" behavioral measures.

On the other hand, it would be possible, though perhaps unlikely, for an ethnographer to conduct research from a logical-positivist stance. For example, imagine a researcher who believes that socioeconomic status is defined solely in terms of material possessions such as televisions, cars, houses, and clothes. Since these material goods can be observed and counted without reference to the meanings that they may have for their owners, such a measure of SES is clearly in the logical-positivist tradition. Then a researcher who uses this measure and who verifies an individual's possessions by ethnographic fieldwork would be subscribing to logical-positivism while using qualitative methods.

• Are qualitative measures necessarily naturalistic, and are quantitative procedures necessarily obtrusive? Qualitative procedures such as participant observation can be obtrusive in some research situations. For example, Margaret Mead's status as an outsider was probably readily detected by the people she chose to study, and this certainly influenced her working relationship with these people. Conversely, some quantitative procedures such as randomized experiments can, on occasion, be used in a completely unobtrusive fashion (cf. Lofland and Lejeune, 1960). In fact, the issue of deception has been raised with many field and laboratory experiments precisely because the researcher and manipulation were thought to be perfectly disguised (cf. Davis, 1961; Lofland, 1961; Roth, 1962; and Kelman, 1972).

• Are qualitative procedures necessarily subjective and quantitative procedures necessarily objective? Following Scriven (1972), one should recognize that the word *subjective* (or alternatively *objective*) has come to possess two separate meanings. Often *subjective* is meant to imply "influenced by human judgment." According to this usage, all methods and measures, both qualitative and quantitative, are subjective. Indeed, modern philosophers of science largely agree that all facts are imbued with theory and so are at least partly subjective. Certainly assigning numbers in a mechanical fashion, as is common in quantitative procedures, does not guarantee objectivity. For example, Bogdan and Taylor (1975) describe an evaluation of a training program which clearly demonstrates the subjectivity of a nominally objective indicator. In that evaluation either a 12% or a 66% success rate could be claimed. The discrepancy arises because of differences in how one (subjectively) chooses to use the objective indicators to define success. Much the same type of subjectivity is involved whenever quantitative design and analysis are employed (cf. Boruch, 1975).

The alternative meaning of *subjective* refers to the measurement of feelings and beliefs. That is, a measure or procedure is subjective if it taps human sentiments—these presumably not being directly observable. Again, there is no reason to assume that qualitative procedures have a monopoly on subjectivity. National surveys of opinion (e.g., a poll of President Carter's popularity) are prime examples of quantitative measures which are subjective. So are the illustrations in the earlier discussion of phenomenologism.

• Do quantitative methods necessarily insulate the researcher from the data? Feinberg (1977: 51) finds it "astonishing that getting close to the data can be thought of as an attribute of only the [qualitative] approach." As an example, Fienberg (1977) tells of sending his graduate students to spend a couple of nights riding around in a patrol car so as to be better able to design a quantitative evaluation of police activities. Similarly, many quantitative researchers venture into the field to "get their hands dirty" and laboratory psychologists will sit through their own manipulations and carefully grill their respondents to find out what their behavioral responses mean. Perhaps a staunch qualitative advocate will claim that these are all examples of quantitative procedures being merged with quantitative methods. Either way, it is clear that the quantitative researcher need not be isolated from the data.

• Are qualitative procedures necessarily grounded, exploratory, and inductive whereas quantitative procedures are always ungrounded, confirmatory, and deductive? Glaser and Strauss (1967: 17-18) are generally acknowledged to have written the Bible on grounded theory. They say: "There is no fundamental clash between the purposes and capacities of qualitative and quantitative methods or data. . . . We believe that *each form of data is useful for both verification and generation of theory,* whatever the primacy of emphasis" (emphasis in the original). We concur: qualitative methods need not only be used to discover which questions are interesting to ask and quantitative procedures need not only be used to answer them. Rather, each procedure can serve each function. For example, Glaser and Strauss (1965, 1967) detail how comparison groups (whether random or otherwise) can be used to great benefit in theory generation. Conversely, qualitative methods have well defined rules of evidence and proof for confirming theories (cf. Barton and Lazarsfeld, 1969; Becker, 1958; and McCall, 1969). Campbell (this volume) not only demonstrates how the ethnographic case study can verify theoretical propositions but offers suggestions for making the procedure better at the task. The point is that the logic of description and inference cuts across methods (cf. Fienberg, 1977). Becker's presentation in this volume makes the same point by applying to one type of qualitative data—photographs—criteria of validity which were originally developed for quantitative methods.

• Must qualitative procedures only be used to measure process, and must quantitative techniques only be used to detect outcome? As with the above distinction between verification and discovery, there need not be a strict division of labor between qualitative and quantitative methods here either. Again, the logic of the task (process discovery versus outcome assessment) cuts across method. Thus, on the one hand, Hollister et al. (this volume) describe process using quantitative techniques, and Campbell (1970) goes so far as to suggest that experimental design would be useful in the study of process because it could help rule out alternative hypotheses. On the other hand, the case study procedure has often been successfully used to assess outcome. For example, a case study is sufficient to detect many of the effects of a flood or hurricane, and the site visit is generally endorsed by the social science profession as an appropriate way to evaluate the effectiveness of training programs.

• Are qualitative methods necessarily valid but unreliable, and are quantitative methods necessarily reliable but invalid? As a counter-example, consider the "participant observation" of a visual illusion. By the very nature of an illusion, observation is bound to produce invalid conclusions which can only be corrected by employing more quantitative procedures (see Campbell's discussion of the Muller-Lyer illusion in this volume). Neither reliability nor validity is an inherent attribute of a measuring instrument (whether this be a ruler or a human eye). Rather, accuracy depends upon the purpose to which the measuring instrument is put and the circumstances under which the measurement is made. Sometimes a person's eyes and ears are the more accurate and meaningful instrument (cf. Brickell, 1976; and Shapiro, 1973), whereas in other cases a more quantitative instrument would be both more valid and reliable.

• Are qualitative methods always limited to the single case and therefore ungeneralizable? Statements that assert the affirmative are wrong on two counts. First, qualitative studies need not be limited to single cases. Rist (1979), for example, reports an ethnographic study which is examining sixty separate sites so as to be better able to generalize. Second, generalizability usually depends on more than sample size. Only in very few cases, such as when using survey sampling with random selection, is generalization from sample data to a population based on statistical reasoning. Usually, generalization is far more informal and therefore much more inductive and potentially fallible. That is, researchers usually want to generalize to populations which have not been sampled (e.g., to children in different school districts, to unemployed heads of households in other cities, and to different times and different types of treatments). Such generalizations are "never fully justified logically" whether based on qualitative or quantitative data (Campbell and Stanley, 1966: 171; also see Cronbach, 1978). While a large and diverse sample of cases can aid in such informal generalizations, so can a depth of understanding of a single case. So in general, there is no reason why quantitative results should be inherently more generalizable than qualitative results.

• Are qualitative procedures necessarily holistic, and are quantitative procedures necessarily particularistic? Clearly, the answer must be negative. A researcher might intensively study only a very circumscribed aspect of behavior using, say, the method of participant observation simply because that behavior is less easily or less accurately observed in any other manner. For example, a subtle behavior may be detectible only by a sophisticated observer who has extensive knowledge of the local culture. In this instance, then, the researcher might use the eye of a participant observer as the measuring instrument yet not be concerned with any wider context than the specific behavior itself. Conversely, quantitative methods such as surveys or randomized experiments can take the "whole picture" into account if by no other means than by measuring "everything."

• Must quantitative procedures assume that reality is stable and unchanging? Granted that some designs are more "rigid" than others, quantitative procedures do not, as a whole, force the investigator to conceive of a fixed reality. Indeed, one of the great advantages of time-series quasi-experiments is that they can track the temporal change in the effect of a program against a background of "natural" changes. Taken to the extreme, no assessment strategy assumes a perfectly fixed reality, since the very purpose of the research is to detect change. This is not to suggest that unplanned and uncontrollable events cannot be hazardous to a successful evaluation; only that changes in the research setting can disturb qualitative as well as quantitative evaluations. For example, the claim is often made that randomized experiments are invalidated when the treatment procedure is altered during the course of the investigation. At the same time, other types of unanticipated change, such as increasing tensions between observer and program staff (see Knapp, this volume), can equally well imperil an ethnographic evaluation. Much can be done in both cases to make evaluations more resilient to undesirable changes.

The Importance of the Situation

From the preceding remarks, we conclude that the attributes of a paradigm are not inherently linked to either qualitative or quantitative methods. Both method-types can be associated with the attributes of either the qualitative or quantitative paradigm. This is not to say that one's paradigmatic stance is unimportant in choosing a method; nor is it to deny that certain methods are usually associated with specific paradigms. The major point is that paradigms are not the sole determinant of the choice of methods.

The choice of research method should also depend at least partly on the demands of the research situation at hand. For example, consider the impact evaluations of two educational programs. In one, the treatment is a new and intensive project aimed at ameliorating the effects of economic disadvantage. The seriousness and relative intransigence of the problem justify a substantial investment of time and money, especially since a program "proven" to be successful might be adopted as a national policy. In this case, a randomized experiment might well be the best means of informing decision makers.

The other educational program is a training grant for graduate study in an academic department. In this case, a large investment of time and money is not warranted, both because the program itself is relatively small and because no national decisions will depend on the outcome of the evaluation. Here, then, a case study technique such as a site visit is the standard procedure. Thus, to advocate that randomized experiments (or site visits) should always be used for impact assessments is as foolish as advocating that they should never be used. In some situations the most efficacious research procedure will be quantitative whereas in others the same research purpose will be best served by a qualitative method.

Wisdom Implicit in the Real but Imperfect
Linkage Between Paradigm and Method

Of course, some wisdom is revealed by the linkage, which exists in practice, between paradigms and methods. Researchers who use qualitative methods do subscribe to the qualitative paradigm more often than to the quantitative paradigm. Similarly, there is a correlation between the use of quantitative methods and adherence to the quantitative paradigm (though these linkages between paradigm and method are not perfect, as many seem to believe). Such linkages may well be the result of an adaptive evaluation reflecting the fact that, all else being equal, qualitative and quantitative methods often are best suited for the separate paradigmatic viewpoints with which they have come to be associated.

We suspect that the most telling and fundamental distinction between the paradigms is on the dimension of verification versus discovery. It appears that quantitative methods have been developed most directly for the task of verifying or confirming theories and that to a large extent qualitative methods were purposely developed for the task of discovering or generating theories. It is hardly surprising then that each method-type would come to be associated with these separate paradigmatic stances and that the methods would also be at their best when used for these specific purposes.

These evolutionary linkages could account for past and recent trends in the use of different methods in evaluation. In the early days, it was assumed that programs could easily be designed to produce desired results and that the purpose of evaluation was merely to verify these anticipated effects. Quite naturally, then, evaluation was drawn toward quantitative methods with their traditional emphasis on verification. Of course, later it was found that amelioration was not so simple and that programs might have a wide variety of unsuspected side effects. The emphasis of evaluation thus began to shift away from the verification of presumed effects toward the discovery both of how a program might be devised so that it would have a desired effect and of what effects either suspected or unsuspected these programs might actually have. Consequently, some fields of evaluation (most notably education) have shown a growing interest in qualitative methods with their emphasis on discovery.

But while the linkage that exists between paradigm and method can usuefully guide one's choice of research method, the linkage should not solely determine that choice. We have argued that the research situation is also an important factor. This is especially important, because evaluation research is conducted under many unique and demanding circumstances which may require modifications in traditional practices. That paradigm and method have been linked in the past does not mean that it is either necessary or wise to do so in the future.

MUST ONE CHOOSE
BETWEEN THE PARADIGMS?

As noted earlier, the current debate over methods creates the impression that the researcher must not only choose a method because of an allegiance to a paradigm but must also choose *between* the qualitative and quantitative paradigms because those are the only choices available. We have discussed the first issue; here we shall deal with second.

The two paradigms under discussion come from two quite different and unique traditions. The conglomerate of attributes that make up the quantitative paradigm grew out of the natural and agricultural sciences, whereas the qualitative paradigm came from work in social anthropology and sociology, particularly the Chicago school. It is not clear why either of these separate traditions would be expected to provide an appropriate paradigm for evaluation research. Fortunately, evaluators are not restricted to these two choices.

Just because one conducts research in a holistic and naturalistic fashion, for example, does not mean that one must adhere to the other attributes of the qualitative paradigm, such as being exploratory and process-oriented. Rather, one could combine the naturalistic and holistic attributes from the qualitative paradigm with other attributes, such as being confirmatory and outcome-oriented, from the quantitative paradigm. Or consider an example from general practice. Logical positivism is no longer a commonly adopted philosophical stance for social research. Most researchers have by now adopted a phenomenological stance whether they combine that with research focusing on process or outcome, naturalism or control.

In fact, all of the attributes which are said to make up the paradigms are logically independent. Just as the methods are not logically linked to any of the paradigmatic attributes, the attributes themselves are not logically linked to each other. We could go through the list of attributes one at a time, as in the previous section, giving examples to demonstrate their independence, but this would soon become tedious. Suffice it to say that there is nothing to stop the researcher, except perhaps tradition, from mixing and matching the attributes from the two paradigms to achieve that combination which is most appropriate for the research problem and setting at hand.

Assuming that considerable evaluation resources are available and that a comprehensive evaluation is desired, one will often want to sample attributes from each paradigm *on the same dimension*. For instance, comprehensive evaluations should be process-oriented as well as outcome-oriented, exploratory as well as confirmatory, and valid as well as reliable. There is no reason for researchers to be constrained to either one of the traditional, though largely arbitrary, paradigms when they can have the best from both.

In addition, evaluators should feel free to change their paradigmatic stance as the need arises. There is no reason to subscribe to one mix of attributes at all times. Rather, in moving from one program to the next or from one study to the next (assuming that a series of evaluations, rather than just a one-shot study, is planned for a single program), the paradigmatic stance that is most appropriate for the research is likely to change. Thus, a researcher's paradigmatic viewpoint should be flexible and adaptive.

WHY NOT USE *BOTH* QUALITATIVE AND QUANTITATIVE METHODS?

Redefining the Debate

We have seen that the choice of methods should not be determined by allegiance to an arbitrary paradigm. This is both because a paradigm is not inherently linked to a set of methods and because the characteristics of the specific research setting are equally as important as the attributes of a paradigm in choosing a method. We have also seen that a researcher need not adhere blindly to one of the polar-extreme paradigms that have been labeled "qualitative" and "quantitative" but can freely choose a mix of attributes from both paradigms so as to best fit the demands of the research problem at hand. There would seem to be, then, no reason to choose *between* qualitative and quantitative *methods* either. Evaluators would be wise to use whatever methods are best suited to their research needs, regardless of the methods' traditional affiliations. If that should call for a combination of qualitative and quantitative methods, then so be it.

Of course, there can still be honest debate over which methods are best *given* a specific paradigmatic view and research situation. For example, some of the literature on manpower training exhibits a disagreement over the likelihood that the income of participants in these programs will change in the absence of a treatment effect. If there is no such maturation (either gain or loss), there is no need for a control group in an impact assessment; a case study design would suffice. On the other hand, if maturation in the absence of the treatment does occur, a control group (perhaps even a random one) would be desirable.

Honest debate can also arise over the appropriateness of a particular paradigmatic stance for a specific evaluation. An example might be a disagreement over the relative importance of internal validity versus generalizability. Certainly both attributes are important; but some evaluators may believe that the best way to achieve generalizability in the long run is to insure that each individual study is internally valid (cf. Campbell, 1969), whereas others may prefer short-run solutions where the immediate goal of generalizability takes precedence over internal validity (cf. Cronbach, 1978).

The problem is that these two legitimate debates are being confused in the literature. Criticisms are being directed at methods when it is really the paradigmatic world view that is under attack, and vice versa. Since methods and paradigms are logically separable, this is a misleading and confusing form of debate. The fact that a method has been poorly used or that it has been used for an inappropriate purpose does not mean that the method itself is faulty or inappropriate. Confusing arguments over paradigms with arguments over methods only leads to the current state of affairs, where researchers are choosing up sides between the method-types. Redefining the debate as two separate and legitimate arguments reveals the fallacy of current ways: rather than being incompatible rivals, the methods can be used together as the research question demands.

A number of researchers have previously advocated this position that qualitative and quantitative methods can be profitably used together, both in the context of evaluation research (cf. Britan, 1978; Campbell, 1974; Cook and Cook, 1977; and Stake, 1978) and in the more traditional substantive disciplines (cf. Denzin, 1970; Eisner, 1977; Erickson, 1977; Rist, 1977; and Sieber, 1973). Perhaps Trow (1957: 338) expressed the sentiment best in a debate over the relative advantages of participant observation compared with interviewing:

> Every cobbler thinks leather is the only thing. Most social scientists, including the present writer, have their favorite research methods with which they are familiar and have some skill in using. And I suspect we mostly choose to investigate problems that seem vulnerable to attack through these methods. But we should at least try to be less parochial than cobblers. Let us be done with the arguments of "participant observation" *versus* interviewing—as we have largely dispensed with the arguments for psychology *versus* sociology—and get on with the business of attacking our problems with the widest array of conceptual and methodological tools that we possess and they demand. This does not preclude discussion and debate regarding the relative usefulness of different methods for the study of specific problems or types of problems. But that is very different from the assertion of the general and inherent superiority of one method over another on the basis of some intrinsic qualities it presumably possesses [emphasis in the original].

Potential Benefits of Using
Qualitative and Quantitative Methods Together

There are at least three reasons that attacking evaluation problems with the most appropriate tools available will result in using a combination of qualitative and quantitative methods. First, evaluation research usually has multiple purposes which must be carried out under the most demanding of conditions. This variety of needs often requires a variety of methods. Second, when used together for the same purpose, the two method-types can build upon each other to offer insights that neither one alone could provide. And third, because all methods have biases, only by using multiple techniques can the researcher triangulate on the underlying truth. Since quantitative and qualitative methods often have different biases, each can be used to check on and learn from the other. While not assuming that these three points are completely unrelated, each will be considered separately below.

(1) Multiple purposes. As previously noted, comprehensive evaluation should be concerned with both process and outcome. By process analysis, researchers have come to reference two different purposes for which we shall give two separate labels. The first meaning of process is monitoring: describing the context and population of the study, discovering the extent to which the treatment or program has been implemented, providing immediate feedback of a formative type, and the like. The second meaning of process is causal explanation: discovering or confirming the process by which the treatment had the effect that it did. Of course, measuring the effect of the program is the summative outcome or impact assessment.

For a complete understanding of the program, an evaluation would have to accomplish at least these three tasks: monitoring, impact assessment, and causal explanation. This is quite a broad range of tasks which, to be most efficaciously met, might well require both qualitative and quantitative methods. Though not inevitable, it might often be the case that monitoring is most efficiently accomplished in a qualitative fashion, impact assessment most accurately performed with quantitative methods, and causal explanation most effectively achieved through the use of qualitative and quantitative methods together. While we certainly want to avoid giving the impression that a rigid or inherent division of labor is required, we believe that more often than not an adaptive and flexible combination of the method-types will be required to accomplish all of an evaluation's purposes.

In using the methods together to satisfy the myriad of research needs, evaluation should be receptive to new and unique forms and concatenations of the methods. It is often said that the quantitative social sciences have adopted their methods wholesale from the natural and agricultural sciences. This would be unfortunate if it were true, since one would hardly expect the tools of one discipline to be best suited for the purposes and circumstances of another. In fact, there has been much refinement of the methods in the process of borrowing them (cf. Boring, 1954, 1969) and new adaptations should be encouraged.

Some useful adaptations may entail a creative marriage of qualitative and quantitative methods, such as using randomized experiments with participant observers as the measuring instruments. This might help avoid the criticism often leveled against quantitative evaluation that the psychometric measures most commonly used are insensitive to the dimension of interest. It might also avoid the criticism leveled against many qualitative evaluations that threats to internal validity are left uncontrolled. For another example, consider the use of ethnographers in combination with the regression-discontinuity design. The essence of the regression-discontinuity design is that the treatment is assigned in strict fashion according to a quantitative dimension (cf. Cook and Campbell, 1979). This could be a measure of geographical distance to a border such as a street or other natural boundary which serves as a cutting line between those who received the treatment and those who did not. To measure the effect of the treatment in such a case, ethnographers could go in and wander freely back and forth across the boundary to determine if there were a discontinuity at that point in the behaviors or attitudes of interest. Other unusual combinations of qualitative and quantitative methods are certainly possible as well.

(2) Each method-type building upon the other. In a fundamental sense, qualitative methods could be defined as techniques of personal understanding, common sense, and introspection whereas quantitative methods could be defined as techniques of counting, scaling, and abstract reasoning. Admittedly, this changes the meanings of qualitative and quantitative methods from what has been used throughout the rest of the chapter though it is justified because some writers do subscribe to these definitions. Such a switch in meaning is useful because the new perspective clearly reveals how each method-type complements the other. Specifically, quantitative knowing must rely on qualitative knowing but in so doing can go beyond it.

Quantitative methods cannot logically replace qualitative methods since quantitative understanding presupposes qualitative knowing. For example, Campbell (this volume) demonstrates how quantitative measurement of a visual illusion is used to correct qualitative observation but does so only by relying on it in many other ways. The basis of the argument is that all measurement is founded on innumerable qualitative assumptions about the nature of the measuring instrument and of the measured reality. For example, in recording the movement of storm fronts, one assumes that the earth's gravitational pull remains constant, since changes would result in an artificial shift in barometric pressure. Or in tracking a child's growth, one assumes that it is the child and not the ruler that is changing over time. In like fashion, qualitative understanding is essential for statistical reasoning. Choosing a statistical model to fit the data, interpreting the results that are output, and generalizing the findings to other settings all rely on qualitative knowing. Quite simply, researchers cannot benefit from the use of numbers if they do not know, in common sense terms, what the numbers mean.

Conversely, qualitative knowing can benefit from quantitative knowing. Even the most introspective and subjectively oriented investigators cannot help but count heads or use such quantitative concepts as "bigger than" and "less than." Quantitative measurement of visual illusions can correct qualitative observation even while relying on it. And a quantitative finding can stimulate further qualitative probing (Light, 1979; and Sieber, 1973), as when a surprising experimental result leads the researcher to question the respondents for introspective clues.

Ordinary science uses qualitative and quantitative knowing together to provide a depth of perception, or a binocular vision, that neither one could provide alone (Eisner, 1977). Far from being antagonistc, the two types of knowing are complementary. This is not to say that combining the two will always be easy. There will often be puzzles which are difficult to solve (cf. Trend, this volume) but there will usually be discrepancies, and therefore puzzles, whenever any two methods are used together. Resolving the puzzles between qualitative and quantitative knowing should be no more difficult in principle than solving other research puzzles, though we suspect that it may often be more enlightening.

(3) Triangulation through converging operations. Using qualitative and quantitative methods in tandem, or, indeed, using any methods together, helps to correct for the inevitable biases that are present in each method. With only one method, it is impossible to separate the bias of the method from the underlying quantity or quality that one is trying to measure. But several methods can be used together to triangulate upon the underlying "truth" separating the wheat from the chaff, so to speak (cf. Denzin, 1970; Garner et al., 1956; and Webb et al., 1966). Whereas any two or more methods can be used for this purpose, disparate methods which still converge on the same operations are better than similar ones because the former are likely to share fewer biases than the latter. Often qualitative and quantitative methods work well together because they are relatively disparate.

In addition, each method-type can potentially teach the other new ways of detecting and reducing bias. Because these two method-types have existed in separate and largely isolated traditions, much of their acquired methodological expertise has been isolated as well. By bringing the methods together, these two separate stores of knowledge and experience can cross-fertilize. Perhaps even new sources of bias and means for their reduction, which were unsuspected by either of the separate traditions alone, will be discovered through their use together.

The tradition in evaluation research has been to focus on quantitative methods, emphasizing both their use and potential biases. Indeed, the fact that many of the likely biases in quantitative methods have been so openly acknowledged has been partly responsible for the growing dissatisfaction with these methods and the increasing advocacy of qualitative methods in some quarters. Certainly the quantitative tradition in evaluation could learn much from the accumulated expertise of bias elimination that has been developed in the qualitative tradition. For example, the qualitative focus on descriptive validity and nonrandom sampling biases (e.g., the elite bias—Vidich and Shapiro, 1955) could well inform quantitative sampling procedures.

Conversely, in spite of the long tradition in the sociological and anthropological literature of anticipating biases, many of the difficulties of using qualitative methods in the context of evaluation research are only beginning to surface (cf. Knapp, this volume; Ianni and Orr, this volume) and this learning process could be speeded by insights gained from the quantitative tradition. For example, quantitative research on the psychological processes of introspection and judgment could well be used to inform the ethnographic observer. Nisbett and Wilson (1977) review the evidence which suggests that observers and participants sometimes cannot accurately describe their own behavior through introspection. Chapman and Chapman's (1967) and Chapman's (1967) research on illusory correlations and Tversky and Kahneman's (1974) work on judgments under uncertainty may help us appreciate biases in the way participant observers detect and record covariation in the behavior under study. Similarly, Scheirer (1978) relies on laboratory research in psychology to suggest that participants, administrators, and observers alike will often over report the positive aspects of a program. In addition, many of the classical ideas of validity associated most strongly with quantitative design can inform the use of qualitative methods as well. Both Becker (this volume) with his concern for ruling out threats to validity in interpreting the qualitative method of photography and Campbell (this volume) with his suggestions for additional comparison groups and multiple observers in case studies are examples.

Obstacles to Using Qualitative and Quantitative Methods Together

Though logically desirable, a number of practical obstacles can stand in the way of combining qualitative and quantitative methods in an evaluation study. The following discussion considers four such constraints.

First, combining qualitative and quantitative methods can be prohibitively expensive. Consider that compared with a case study, a randomized experiment has the additional expense of having to collect data from an untreated control group, while the data collection costs per respondent for the ethnographic fieldworker are usually far greater than for the "standard" survey questionnaire of quantitative procedures. Combining the two methods may end up concatenating the relatively more costly elements of each.

Second, using qualitative and quantitative methods together may take too much time. Proponents on both sides of the debate over method-types worry that their preferred methods may be too slow for political deadlines. Randomized experiments, for example, have to allow enough time, between assigning respondents to conditions and collecting posttest data, for the treatment to run its course. Similarly, ethnographers need sufficient time to develop rapport, explore freely those aspects of the program that seem relevant, and follow up on leads that thereby arise, and then need again as much time to synthesize their field notes into a final report. In either case, this could take years. Unless the activities of the two methods can proceed concurrently, there simply may not be enough time to use both.

Third, researchers may not have sufficient training in both method-types to do both. Most studies that combine the two method-types will usually have to rely on interdisciplinary teams. When the members of the team come from the separate traditions of qualitative and quantitative methods, the interplay between the two factions does not always run smoothly (see Ianni and Orr, this volume; and Trend, this volume).

Finally, there is the matter of faddism and the adherence to the dialectical form of the debate. Evaluation, like science generally, suffers from fads. With good cause, researchers are often reluctant to be out of vogue, especially when funding agencies are participants in the current trend. Such trends often favor one or the other of the method-types but seldom value both equally. It will be difficult to convince researchers to combine the method-types until the illogic of the current debate, with its separatist theme, is made clear.

For these reasons, we are not optimistic that the joint use of qualitative and quantitative methods will become commonplace. This does not mean that evaluators should return to choosing one set or the other based on paradigmatic dogma. Evaluators should still fit the methods to the demands of the research problem in the best manner possible, regardless of traditional paradigmatic affiliations. It does mean, however, that evaluators will have to establish a priority of purposes and questions since they will usually be unable to meet all the desired goals. Often we suspect that the question of impact will have highest priority and that quantitative procedures will be given precedence. But whatever, employing only one or the other of the method-types will usually mean accepting a noncomprehensive evaluation.

CONCLUSION

Much good has come from the recent debate over the use of qualitative and quantitative methods in evaluation research. Many evaluators who were raised in the quantitative tradition (including the present authors) have been overly zealous in their use of quantitative *methods*, much like Trow's cobbler who sees everything in leather or the child who, when first given a hammer, finds that everything needs hammering. In response, the debate has made clear that quantitative methods are not always best suited for some of the research purposes and settings in which they have been used. The debate has appropriately helped to legitimize and increase the use of qualitative methods in evaluation.

Many evaluators have also been too quick to embrace the set of attributes that make up the quantitative *paradigm*. In response, the debate has focused attention on process, discovery, closeness to the data, holism, naturalism, and the other attributes of the qualitative paradigm. In the past the pendulum has swung too far toward the quantitative side in both paradigm and method and the debate has awakened evaluators to this imbalance.

But while the debate has served a very useful purpose, it has also been partly dysfunctional. In large part, the way the debate is currently being argued serves to polarize the qualitative and quantitative positions and to foster the belief that the *only* available option is a choice *between* these two extremes. It is as if the pendulum must swing to either one side or the other. The currently perceived overemphasis on quantitative methods can then only be corrected by an equal but opposite emphasis on qualitative methods. Of course, once qualitative methods have been put to the test as thoroughly as quantitative procedures have been in the past, the qualitative methods will be found to be just as fallible and feeble (see Overholt and Stallings, 1979). If the dichotomization between the methods is maintained, the pendulum will swing back toward quantitative procedures in an inevitable backlash. Undoubtedly this too would be found unsatisfactory, so the pendulum would swing back again, and so on. Thus the current debate keeps the pendulum swinging between extremes of methods and extremes of dissatisfaction.

The solution, of course, is to realize that the debate is inappropriately stated. There is no need to choose a research method on the basis of a traditional paradigmatic stance. Nor is there any reason to pick between two polar-opposite paradigms. Thus, there is no need for a dichotomy between the method-types and there is every reason (at least in logic) to use them together to satisfy the demands of evaluation research in the most efficacious manner possible.

Hopefully, the next generation of evaluators will be trained in both the qualitative and quantitative traditions. These researchers will be able to use the broadest possible range of methods and will tailor the techniques to research problems without parochialism. They will learn new ways of combining the methods and of reconciling discrepant findings without arbitrarily rejecting one set in favor of the other. These evaluators will also be modest in their claims about methods. They will realize that all methods are fallible and that the discovery of a bias is not necessarily a reason to reject a method but a challenge to improve it, just as we strive to improve a theory in the face of disconfirming data. Acquiring these skills will be no easy task, but it will be well worth the effort.

Undoubtedly, there is some pedogogical advantage to the dialectic form of argument that polarizes qualitative and quantitative methods. For example, it is often easiest to state a case by dichotomizing a continuum into polar extremes so that the dimension of interest is more clearly revealed. But the lesson that quantitative methods can be overused has already been learned, and it is now time to stop the pendulum from swinging from one extreme to the other. It is time to stop building walls between the methods and start building bridges. Perhaps it is even time to go beyond the dialectic language of qualitative and quantitative methods. The real challenge is to fit the research methods to the evaluation problem without parochialism. This may well call for a combination of qualitative and quantitative methods. To distinguish between the two by using separate labels may serve only to polarize them unnecessarily. Leaving the labels behind, we would have no choice but to go beyond the debate of qualitative versus quantitative methods.

OVERVIEW OF VOLUME

In putting together the readings for the present volume, a diversity of opinion on the use of qualitative and quantitative methods was purposely sought. In part, diversity was achieved by selecting authors who were known to represent divergent views. For example, Becker (Becker and Geer, 1957) and Filstead (1970) are well known advocates of qualitative methods whereas Campbell (Campbell and Stanley, 1966) has long been considered a supporter of quantitative methods. Diversity was also achieved by sampling authors from a wide variety of substantive disciplines. The fields of anthropology, economics, education, psychology, and sociology are each represented by at least two authors (or coauthors).

The result is that different chapters exhibit strongly held preferences for different methods. The dissension that is present, however, is less extreme than might be expected. Even in those chapters with the most extreme preferences for *one or the other* of the method-types, there is still a sense that *both* qualitative and quantitative methods are required for a comprehensive evaluation. In other words, there is agreement that neither method-type alone is generally sufficient for all of the diverse requirements of evaluation research. Perhaps the debate *between* the methods is indeed starting to undergo a redefinition.

The chapters have been ordered in the volume starting with those most adamant and ending with those most cautious in their support of qualitative methods. In this regard, Filstead's chapter is a most appropriate lead. Filstead distinguishes the traditionally held differences between the qualitative and quantitative paradigms and forcefully argues that it is the qualitative paradigm (with its belief in social reality as constructed by the participants and its emphasis on understanding events from the perspective of the actors themselves) that is most appropriate for evaluation research. Filstead also presents reasons why the mood among educational evaluators, for example, is shifting from an overemphasis on quantitative methods to an appreciation of qualitative techniques. To speed this change, Filstead suggests how qualitative methods can be better used to inform evaluation research.

In what will perhaps be surprisng to some evaluators, but certainly not all, Campbell's contribution provides a convincing rationale for the use of qualitative methods in the case study design. Exhibiting a change in sentiment (and background assumptions) from earlier papers, Campbell argues that the case study can possess sufficient discipline (because of "degrees of freedom coming from multiple implications of any one theory") to both confirm and infirm causal hypotheses. Campbell also demonstrates the inherent complementarity of qualitative and quantitative methods by describing how quantitative knowing only goes beyond qualitative knowing by relying on it. Nonetheless, Campbell remains convinced that the case study is still highly susceptible to bias when used to assess program impact.

He also suggests several steps that can be taken to reduce but not eliminate that equivocality.

The article by Trend is perhaps best described as a detective story. The author reports on his experiences in an evaluation of a major housing allowance demonstration which used both participant observers and questionnaire surveys. In one site in particular, these two data sources produced highly discrepant findings leading to considerable controversy among the analysts. Working with both sources, Trend solves the puzzle and documents how the resulting synthesis goes well beyond the original reports in offering insight into the data. Trend argues that discrepant findings should be encouraged initially so that significant paths of investigation are not closed off prematurely.

Ianni and Orr's major point is that evaluators can profitably use ethnographic techniques only if these methods are carefully adapted to fit the unique demands of evaluation research. Ianni and Orr see a number of pressures leading to the increased use of qualitative methods in educational evaluation but suggest that, at present, these methods are often being used inappropriately. They argue that the use of these methods must be guided by theory and that the theory of the traditional social science disciplines is not adequate for evaluation purposes. Suggestions are offered for developing a conceptual framework for evaluation that is appropriate.

Admittedly, the inclusion of Becker's article may appear to be a bit unusual. In this case, however, appearances are deceptive. While the article is ostensibly concerned with photography, Becker's thoughts also have great relevance for the use of ethnographic methods in evaluation. The point is that photographs are similar to any piece of data and, in particular, they have much in common with data collected by qualitative procedures. So just as Becker is concerned with the "truth" of a photograph, so too qualitative evaluators should be concerned with the validity of their data. Of greatest significance is that Becker uses the logic of Campbell and Stanley (1966), which was originally developed in reference to quantitative methods, to evaluate the validity of inferences about photographs. Thus, Becker demonstrates that ruling out rival hypotheses follows the same logic in both qualitative and quantitative procedures. Becker also has much to say about generalizability, observer bias, and censorship and editing.

Knapp provides a well-reasoned and insightful examination of the use of ethnography in the evaluation of the Experimental Schools Program. In documenting the many difficulties that emerged, Knapp leads one to appreciate both the subtle and not-so-subtle corrupting pressures that large-scale evaluations exert on ethnographic fieldwork. Those who believe that successful ethnography is easily carried out in large-scale evaluations will be rudely awakened, and those who would use ethnography would be well advised to understand the dilemmas that Knapp documents. Similarly, one is encouraged to consider Knapp's recommendations for alternative uses of ethnography in evaluation research.

Finally, Hollister et al. offer some novel insights into the use of quantitative methods. Current thinking in evaluation research suggests that process analysis requires qualitative procedures whereas outcome assessment demands quantitative techniques. Hollister et al. debunk this myth by demonstrating not only that both process and outcome analyses can be performed with "standard" quantitative methods, but, more importantly, how these two analyses can be linked together. Although such linked analyses require data of great breadth and quality, Hollister et al. reveal the potential benefits that these analyses have to offer.

REFERENCES

BARTON, A. H. and P. F. LAZARSFELD (1969) "Some functions of qualitative analysis in social research," in G. J. McCall and J. L. Simmons (eds.) Issues in Participant Observation: A Text and Reader. Reading, MA: Addison-Wesley.

BECKER, H. S. (1958) "Problems of inference and proof in participant observation." American Sociological Review 169: 652-660.

——— and B. GEER (1957) "Participant observation and interviewing: a comparison." Human Organization 16: 28-32.

BOGDAN, R. and S. TAYLOR (1975) Introduction to Qualitative Research Methods. New York: John Wiley.

BORING, E. G. (1969) "Perspective: artifact and control," in R. Rosenthal and R. L. Rosnow (eds.) Artifact in Behavioral Research. New York: Academic Press.

——— (1954) "The nature and history of experimental control." American Journal of Psychology 67: 573-589.

BORUCH, R. F. (1975) "On common contentions about randomized experiments for evaluating social programs," in R. F. Boruch and H. W. Riecken (eds.) Experimental Testing of Public Policy. Boulder: Westview.

BRICKELL, H. M. (1976) "Needed: instruments as good as our eyes." Journal of Curriculum Evaluation 2: 56-66.

BRITAN, G. M. (1978) "Experimental and contextual models of program evaluation." Evaluation and Program Planning 1: 229-234.

CAMPBELL, D. T. (1974) "Qualitative knowing in action research." Kurt Lewin Award Address, Society for the Psychological Study of Social Issues, meeting with the American Psychological Association, New Orleans, September 1. (to appear, after revision, in Journal of Social Issues)

——— (1970) "Considering the case against experimental evaluations of social innovations." Administrative Science Quarterly 15: 110-113.

——— (1969) "Artifact and control," in R. Rosenthal and R. L. Rosnow (eds.) Artifact in Behavioral Research. New York: Academic Press.

—— and J. C. STANELY (1966) Experimental and Quasi-Experimental Designs for Research. Chicago: Rand McNally.

CHAPMAN, L. J. (1967) "Illusory correlation in observational report." Journal of Verbal Learning and Verbal Behavior 6: 151-155.

—— and J. P. CHAPMAN (1967) "Genesis of popular but erroneous psychodiagnostic observations." Journal of Abnormal Psychology 72: 193-204.

COOK, T. D. and D. T. CAMPBELL (1979) Quasi-Experimentation: Design and Analysis Issues for Field Settings. Chicago: Rand McNally.

COOK, T. D. and F. L. COOK (1977) "Comprehensive evaluation research and its dependence on both humanistic and empiricist perspectives," in R. S. French (ed.) Humanists and Policy Studies: Relevance Revisited: Curriculum Development in the Humanities, No. 3. Washington, DC: George Washington University, Division of Experimental Programs.

CRONBACH, L. J. (1978) "Designing educational evaluations." Stanford: Stanford University. (unpublished)

DAVIS, F. (1961) "Comment on 'Initial interaction of newcomers in Alcoholics Anonymous.'" Social Problems 8: 364-365.

DENZIN, N. (1970) The Research Act. Chicago: Aldine.

EISNER, E. W. (1977) "Critique." Anthropology and Education Quarterly 8: 71-72.

ERICKSON, F. (1977) "Some approaches to inquiry in school-community ethnography." Anthropology and Education Quarterly 8: 58-69.

FIENBERG, S. E. (1977) "The collection and analysis of ethnographic data in educational research." Anthropology and Education Quarterly 8: 50-57.

FILSTEAD, W. J. [ed.] (1970) Qualitative Methodology. Chicago: Markham.

GARNER, W. R., H. W. HAKE, and C. W. ERICKSEN (1956) "Operationism and the concept of perception." Psychological Review 63: 149-159.

GLASER, B. and A. L. STRAUSS (1967) The Discovery of Grounded Theory. Chicago: Aldine.

—— (1965) "Discovery of substantive theory: a basic strategy underlying qualitative research." American Behavioral Scientist 8: 5-12.

GUBA, E. G. (1978) Toward a Methodology of Naturalistic Inquiry in Educational Evaluation. Los Angeles: University of California, Los Angeles, Center for the Study of Evaluation.

KELMAN, H. C. (1972) "The rights of the subject in social research: an analysis in terms of relative power and legitimacy." American Psychologist 27: 989-1016.

KUHN, T. S. (1970) The Structure of Scientific Revolutions. Chicago: University of Chicago Press.

—— (1962) The Structure of Scientific Revolutions. Chicago: University of Chicago Press.

LIGHT, R. (1979) "Integrating multiple empirical studies." Presented at the American Educational Research Association annual meeting, San Francisco.

LOFLAND, J. (1961) "Reply to Davis' comment on 'Initial interaction.'" Social Problems 8: 365-367.

—— and R. A. LEJEUNE (1960) "Initial interaction of newcomers in Alcoholics Anonymous: a field experiment in class symbols and socialization." Social Problems 8: 102-11.

McCALL, G. J. (1969) "The problem of indicators in participant observation research," in G. J. McCall and J. L. Simmons (eds.) Issues in Participant Observation: A Text and Reader. Reading, MA: Addison-Wesley.

NISBETT, R. E. and T. D. WILSON (1977) "Telling more than we can know: verbal reports on mental processes." Psychological Review 84: 231-259.

OVERHOLT, G. E. and W. M. STALLINGS (1979) "Ethnography in evaluation: dangers of methodological transplant." Presented at the American Educational Research Association annual meeting, San Francisco.

PARLETT, M. and D. HAMILTON (1976) "Evaluation as illumination: a new approach to the study of innovatory programs," in G. V Glass (ed.) Evaluation Studies: Review Annual, Vol. 1. Beverly Hills: Sage.

PATTON, M. Q. (1978) Utilization-Focused Evaluation. Beverly Hills: Sage.

——— (1975) Alternative Evaluation Research Paradigm. Grand Forks: University of North Dakota Press.

RIECKEN, W. R., R. F. BORUCH, D. T. CAMPBELL, N. CAPLAN, T. K. GLENAN, Jr., J. W. PRATT, A. REES, and W. WILLIAMS (1974) Social Experimentation: A Method for Planning and Evaluating Social Intervention. New York: Academic Press.

RIST, R. C. (1979) "On the utility of ethnographic case studies for federal policy." Presented at the American Educational Research Association annual meeting, San Francisco.

——— (1977) "On the relations among educational research paradigms: from disdain to detente." Anthropology and Education Quarterly 8: 42-49.

ROSSI, P. H. and S. R. WRIGHT (1977) "Evaluation research: an assessment of theory, practice, and politics." Evaluation Quarterly 1: 5-52.

ROTH, J. A. (1962) "Comments on 'Secret observation.'" Social Problems 9: 283-284.

SCHEIRER, M. A. (1978) "Program participants' positive perceptions: psychological conflict of interest in social program evaluation." Evaluation Quarterly 2: 53-70.

SCRIVEN, M. (1972) "Objectivity and subjectivity in educational research," in L. G. Thomas (ed.) Philosophical Redirection of Educational Research: The Seventy-first Yearbook of the National Society for the Study of Education. Chicago: University of Chicago Press.

SHAPIRO, E. (1973) "Educational evaluation: rethinking the criterion of competence." School Review 81: 523-549.

SIEBER, S. (1973) "The integration of field work and survey methods." American Journal of Sociology 28: 1335-1359.

STAKE, R. E. (1978) "Should educational evaluation be more objective or more subjective? More subjective!" Invited debate at the American Educational Research Association annual meeting.

TROW, M. (1957) "Comment on 'Participant observation and interviewing: a comparison." Human Organization 16: 33-35.

TVERSKY, A. and D. KAHNEMAN (1974) "Judgments under uncertainty: heuristics and biases." Science 185: 1124-1131.

VIDICH, A. J. and G. SHAPIRO (1955) "A comparison of participant observation and survey data." American Sociological Review 20: 28-33.

WEBB, E. J., D. T. CAMPBELL, R. D. SCHWARTZ, and L. SECHREST (1966) Unobtrusive Measures: Nonreactive Research in the Social Sciences. Chicago: Rand McNally.

WEISS, R. S. and M. REIN (1972) "The evaluation of broad-aim programs: difficulties in experimental design and an alternative," in C. H. Weiss (ed.) Evaluating Action Programs: Readings in Social Action and Education. Boston: Allyn and Bacon.

WILSON, S. (1977) "The use of ethnographic techniques in educational research." Review of Educational Research 47: 245-265.

William J. Filstead
Northwestern University

2

QUALITATIVE METHODS
A Needed Perspective
in Evaluation Research

The role of qualitative methods either alone or in conjunction with quantitative methods has attracted the attention of various publics associated with administrating and evaluating social intervention programs. The literature in this area has its beginnings in the late sixties, when examples of the use of qualitative methods in evaluation research first appeared (cf. Mech, 1969; Glaser, 1969). Recently, other publications have appeared which provide conceptual frameworks (Campbell, 1974; Brenner et al., 1978; Britan, 1978; Patton, 1978; and Hamilton et al., 1977) and procedural suggestions (Tikunoff and Ward, 1977; and Sobel, 1976) for using these methods in evaluation research. In contrast, the role of qualitative methods has not been addressed in any detail by the standard textbooks and anthologies on evaluation (see Caro, 1971; Rossi and Williams, 1972; Attkisson et al., 1978; Coursey et al., 1977; Struening and Guttentag, 1975; and Riecken and Boruch, 1974).

The purposes of this chapter are threefold: (1) to compare and contrast the qualitative and quantitative styles of research; (2) to discuss what factors have led to a heightened interest in qualitative methods for evaluating the impact of social intervention programs; and (3) to suggest ways in which qualitative methods can be used in evaluation research. While both qualitative and quantitative paradigms are considered, the presentation emphasizes the former. This is done in part because those who read this chapter will by and large already have extensive training in the quantitative paradigm. They will know what to read if they wish to expand upon the observations that are made about that framework. Conversely, most behavioral scientists have not received comparable training in qualitative methods. If anything has been learned about this paradigm, it usually has been the result of a lecture or two in a graduate-level research course, though perhaps a few of the readers will have extensive training in this orientation. In addition, I openly promote the advantages of the qualitative paradigm in order to affect the imbalance which now exists in the evaluation field. It is hoped that by viewing these paradigms as opposites, productive efforts can be mounted to devise procedures for incorporating their respective assets into future evaluation efforts.

THE QUALITATIVE AND QUANTITATIVE PARADIGMS

The phrases *qualitative methods* and *quantitative methods* mean far more than specific data-collecting techniques. They are more appropriately conceptualized as paradigms. A paradigm, as defined by Kuhn (1962), is a set of interrelated assumptions about the social world which provides a philosophical and conceptual framework for the organized study of that world.

According to Kuhn, the day-to-day work of science (in our case evaluation research) is organized around a paradigm.[1] In its broadest sense, a paradigm represents a "disciplinary matrix" which encompasses the commonly shared generalizations, assumptions, values, beliefs, and examples of what constitutes the discipline's interest (Kuhn, 1970: 181-187). A paradigm (1) serves as a guide to the professionals in a discipline, for it indicates what are the important problems and issues confronting the discipline; (2) goes about developing an explanatory scheme (i.e., models and theories) which can place these issues and problems in a framework which will allow practitioners to try to solve them; (3) establishes the criteria for the appropriate "tools" (i.e., methodologies, instruments, and types and forms of data collection) to use in solving these disciplinary puzzles; and (4) provides an epistemology in which the preceding tasks can be viewed as organizing principles for carrying out the "normal work" of the discipline. Paradigms not only allow a discipline to "make sense" of different kinds of phenomena but provide a framework in which these phenomena can be identified as existing in the first place. In a very real sense, to understand a paradigm one must understand the processes by which it was "discovered"—that is, how the paradigm came to be *the* way of viewing a given phenomenon.

At the heart of the distinction between the quantitative and qualitative paradigms lies the classic argument in philosophy between the schools of realism and idealism, and their subsequent reformulations (see Aiken, 1957; Coser, 1971; Becker and Barnes, 1952; Polanyi, 1958; Popper, 1972; Quine, 1969; and Feyerabend, 1975). The writings of Hobbes, Locke, Bacon, Kant, Berkeley, Hume, and others focused on, among other things, the relation between the external world and the process of knowing. The essential question with which they were concerned was: How do we know what we know? The continuing debate surrounding this question highlights the sets of assumptions underlying our view of the world which to a great extent shape the world we see.

The birth of science in the fifteenth and sixteenth centuries was made possible by an essentially static conception of the world that dominated the thinking of men of ideas. There was faith in reason as the way of understanding the world, and this reason eventually became based on a faith in science. The world was held to be capable of understanding through man's senses. As a result, science was proclaimed to be the way of understanding the world. The Baconian reality of "I see it because I experience it" sums up the thrust of thinking which became known as realism and logical positivism.

Turmoil and rapid social change in the institutions of society during the eighteenth and nineteenth centuries caused scholars to question the logic and method of science as it applied to understanding human beings. This was particularly true of the German idealists who acknowledged the existence of a physical reality but held that the mind was the source and creator of knowledge. They believed that the social world is not given but is created by the individuals who live in it.

It is the clash with respect to these basic philosophical stances toward the nature of the social order which distinguishes quantitative and qualitative paradigms. The quantitative paradigm's approach to social life employs the mechanistic and static assumptions of the natural science positivist model. Specifically the quantitative paradigm is based on the following assumptions:

> First, the positivists assume that scientists can, almost automatically, attain objective knowledge of the study of both the social and natural worlds. Second, they argue that the natural and social sciences share a basic methodology, that they are similar, not by virtue of their subject matter, but because they employ the same logic of inquiry and similar research procedures. . . . Third, the positivists, unlike the writers in the neo-idealist tradition, generally think of a mechanistic natural and social order [Sjoberg and Nett, 1966: 7].

On the other hand, the qualitative paradigm has the decidedly humanistic cast to understanding social reality of the idealist position which stresses an evolving, negotiated view of the social order. The qualitative paradigm perceives social life as the shared creativity of individuals. It is this sharedness which produces a reality perceived to be objective, extant, and knowable to all participants in social interaction. Furthermore, the social world is not fixed or static but shifting, changing, dynamic. The qualitative paradigm does not conceive of the world as an external force, objectively identifiable and independent of man. Rather, there are multiple realities. In this paradigm individuals are conceptualized as active agents in constructing and making sense of the realities they encounter rather than responding in a robotlike fashion according to role expectations established by social structures. There exist no clear-cut response-sets to situations, but instead an agreed upon pattern of interaction emerges through a negotiated and interpretative process. The qualitative paradigm also includes an assumption about the importance of understanding situations from the perspective of the participants in the situation.

The basic starting point of the qualitative paradigm in conceptualizing the social world is the development of concepts and theories that are grounded in the data (i.e., concepts and theories derived from the data and illustrated by characteristic examples of the data; Glaser and Strauss, 1967). These "first order concepts," as Schutz (1967) called them, are essential to the development of second order concepts, that is, concepts which emerge in attempting to explain a phenomenon.

> Any scientific understanding of human action, at whatever level of ordering or generality, must begin with and be built upon an understanding of the everyday life of the members performing those actions. To fail to see this and to act in accord with it is to commit what we might call the fallacy of abstractionism, that is, the fallacy of believing that you can know in a more abstract form what you do not know in a particular form [Douglas, 1970: 11].

It is precisely this focus on the social meanings and the insistence that these meanings can only be examined in the context of individuals interacting that distinguishes this paradigm from the natural science model of inquiry. As Erickson (1977): 50) has stated,

> Researchers of the Malinowski tradition in anthropology (and "field work sociologists," "symbolic interactionists," and more recently "ethnomethodogists," in sociology) have been concerned with *social fact* as *social action;* with *social meanings* as residing in and constituted by people's *doing* in everyday life. These meanings are most often discovered through field work by hanging around and watching people carefully and asking them why they do what they do, sometimes asking them as they are in the midst of their doing. Because of this orientation toward social as embedded in the concrete, particular doings of people—doings that include people's intentions and points of view—qualitative researchers are reluctant to see attributes of doing abstracted from the scene of social action and counted out of context.

Erickson (1977: 61) goes on to describe the basic analytical strategy behind qualitative methods. "What qualitative research does best and most essentially is to describe key incidents in functionally relevant descriptive terms and place them in some relation to the wider social context, using the key incident as a concrete instance of the workings of abstract principles of social organization."

Because of the assumptions that the quantitative paradigm makes about social life and the approach it takes toward comprehending social life, it has been unable to provide the context within which to "make sense," "understand," and therefore arrive at the meaning of the interactions and processes it has been examining. One cannot infer the meaning of an event from data that does not have this dimension of information. A characterization of social life devoid of the subjective meaning of these events to the participants does violence to the image of man which portrays him as not only a reactor but a creator of his world.

Each paradigm attempts to convey the information it obtains through a written notation system. Quantitative researchers tend to translate their observations into numbers. Numerical values are assigned to the observations via counting and "measuring." Qualitatively inclined researchers rarely assign numerical values to their observations but prefer instead to record their data in the language of their subjects. The actual words of the subjects are thought to be critical to the process of conveying the meaning systems of the participants which eventually become the results or findings of the research.

More often than not, the researcher in the quantitative paradigm is concerned with discovering, verifying, or identifying causal relationships among concepts that derive from an a priori theoretical scheme. The assignment of subjects is of concern, and efforts are generally taken to use either random assignment or other sampling techniques to minimize intervening variables which could impact the results of the research. Often a "control group" is used for purposes of evaluating the "impact" of no intervention. Data is collected via established procedures such as structured questionnaires and interviews designed to capture subject responses to predetermined questions with established response options. Statistical procedures of varying complexities are employed to analyze this information. Blumer (1969: 24) in characterizing such current methodological approaches in sociology made the following observation (which is also applicable to the general tenor of contemporary evaluation research):

Today "methodology" in the social sciences is regarded with depressing frequency as synonymous with the study of advanced quantitative procedures and a "methodologist" is one who is expertly versed in the knowledge and use of such procedures. He is generally viewed as someone who casts a study in terms of quantifiable variables, who seeks to establish relations between such variables by the use of sophisticated statistical and mathematical techniques, and who guides such study by elegant logical models conforming to "special canons" of "research design." Such conceptions are a travesty on methodology as the logical study of the principles underlying the conduct of scientific inquiry.

By way of contrast, a qualitative researcher, while being aware of existing theoretical frameworks or explanation schemes for the phenomenon under study, prefers the "theory" to emerge from the data itself. This grounding of theory in data, as discussed above, enhances the ability of the researcher to understand and perhaps ultimately devise an explanation of the phenomenon which is consistent with its occurrence in the social world. By attempting to ground the theory, the researcher attempts to find out what explanation schemes are used by the subjects under study to make sense of the social realities they encounter; what theories, concepts, and categories are suggested by the data itself. The insistence upon this closeness to the everyday worlds of the participants and to comprehending their actions in situ gives a strong underpinning to the explanations which the research eventually develops. These explanations do in fact explain or make sense because of the very fact that they were generated through a process which tapped the participants' perspectives.

In developing the "explanations" of the phenomenon, the qualitative researcher tends to make use of "sensitizing concepts" (i.e., concepts which capture the meaning of events and use descriptions of these events to clarify the multiple facets of the concept, Blumer, 1969) rather than operational definitions. Whom one selects to study, while initially guided by the research question, undergoes changes based on what data are being collected and the direction such information suggests with respect to who can provide additional information to answer emerging questions that were generated by this research process. This style of subject selection has been called "theoretical sampling" (Glaser and Strauss, 1967). The data gathering techniques typically used for these purposes are participant observation, in-depth interviewing, and unstructured or semistructured interviewing. There is a substantial body of literature, primarily in anthropology and sociology, which provides descriptions of the underlying assumptions, specific techniques, strategies of using such methods, and other refinements and nuances in the approach and use of qualitative methods (e.g., Bruyn, 1966; Lofland, 1973, 1976; McCall and Simmons, 1969; Becker, 1970; Filstead, 1970, 1973, 1975, 1976, 1978; Bogdan and Taylor, 1975; Bogdan, 1972; Junker, 1960; and Schwartz and Jacobs, 1979).

In sum, the quantitative paradigm employs a lock-step model of logicodeductive reasoning from theory to propositions, concept formation, operational definition, measurement of the operational definitions, data collection, hypotheses testing, and analysis. The qualitative paradigm is a dynamic interchange between theory, concepts, and data with constant feedback and modifications of theory and concepts based on the data collected. This emerging, refined "explanation framework" gives direction to where additional data need to be collected. It is marked by a concern with the discovery of theory rather than the verification of theory.

THE CHANGING CLIMATE
OF EVALUATION RESEARCH

The blanket acceptance of the quantitative paradigm as *the* model for evaluation research is being seriously questioned by the evaluation research community. This questioning has given rise to a changing climate, the present volume being one indication of the shifting sentiment. At least three factors have contributed to this reconsideration of the nature of evaluation research.

The first factor, while it does not directly emanate from evaluation research per se, created the climate which allowed a rethinking of "Why are things done the way they are?" Only within the last decade has it become possible to study science as other aspects of our society are studied. Science has lost its aura of eliteness and sacredness, which in the past has prevented researchers from questioning its assumptions. No knowledge, be it scientific or commonsensical, is or can be completely free of human interest, that is, devoid of relevancy. Believing this leads one to seek to understand what human interests and events interact to shape knowledge (Haberman, 1971). It is a switch from the perspective of science and the knowledge it yields as being revealed to us to the perspective which sees science and its knowledge as being socially created by individuals and events which has shaped the kinds of questions science asks and the procedures for arriving at information to answer these questions. (See Barnes and Shapin, 1979; and Mitroff, 1974).

The second factor is that the payoff of quantitative program evaluations to program administrators and bureaucrats has been far less than anticipated. Administrators had expected these types of evaluations to identify "what works," "who gets better," "what areas to change," and so on. These expectations have not been generally met.

Administrators' expectations for definitive answers regarding a social intervention's impact may have been unrealistic, but they were fostered and supported by the advocates of the quantitative model of evaluation and the taken-for-granted assumptions about the appropriateness of the natural science framework to program evaluation activities. For example, Campbell and Stanley (1966: 2), in their discussion of the central role played by experimentation in the verification and cumulation of knowledge, state that experimentation represents: "the only means of settling disputes regarding educational practice, the only way of verifying educational improvement, and the only way of establishing a cumulative tradition in which improvements can be introduced without the danger of a faddish discard of old wisdom in favor of inferior novelties."

Following the influx of the "Great Society Programs" of the 60s and early 70s, and their spinoffs, there came the call for assessing the impact of these programs. The evaluation business became a respectable endeavor (although generally not in academic settings), and it became one ideally suited for social and behavioral scientists. The tools of the scientific method were applied rigorously because the political climate had been created in which the positive impact of these programs was assumed, but had to be empirically established. The option of being committed to finding out the relative impact of various interventions was not available (Campbell, 1969, 1971). The tools of the scientific method plus its principles of rigor, objectivity, definitiveness, and so forth represented a needed commodity to program administrators and bureaucrats. The quantitative model was looked upon as the only way to definitively know the (already assumed) positive impact of such programs.

Given this climate, it is little wonder that so much allegiance was given this approach to program evaluation. Consequently, where the outcomes of these evaluations were ambiguous, or, worse, negative, and the mode and style of feedback difficult and at times impossible to comprehend, a sense of disenchantment with these approaches started to develop. As I have indicated elsewhere (Filstead, 1978), evaluations result in only three types of impacts: a positive impact, an unclear or ambiguous impact, and a negative impact. With the results of many social interventions yielding unclear or negative impacts, bureaucrats began to distrust such evaluation approaches because they did not have potential benefit to their organizations. Furthermore, underlying these concerns was a growing belief that these types of quantitative evaluations really did not capture the "experience" or the "essence" of the intervention program under study. That is to say, program administrators often felt the evaluation effort achieved only an incomplete comprehension of the social intervention.

The third reason for this changing climate in evaluation research is that many evaluators are questioning the conceptual model of standard quantitative program evaluations and are looking for either alternative models or models that incorporate multiple methods.

At the heart of the conflict over appropriate conceptual models for evaluation research is a fundamental disagreement about the "causal-problem-solving" posture of the scientific method. Evaluators who employ this causal-problem-solving model in studying a social intervention program adhere to the following type of thinking which Patton (1975: 29) described in an educational research context:

> Treatments in educational research are usually some type of new hardware, or specific curriculum innovation, variation in class size, or some specific type of teaching style. One of the main problems in experimental educational research is clear specification of what the treatment actually is, which infers controlling all other possible causal variables and the corresponding problem of multiple treatment interference and interactive effects. It is the constraints posed by controlling the specific treatment under study that necessitate

simplifying and breaking down the totality of reality into small component parts. A great deal of the scientific enterprise revolves around this process of simplifying the complexity of reality.

It is precisely this fragmentation or compartmentalized style of evaluation which qualitatively oriented evaluators argue leads to distortions of reality and, as a consequence, necessitates a holistic or contextual model of evaluation (see Britan, 1978; Weiss and Rein, 1972).

> Focusing on a narrow set of variables necessarily sets up a filtering screen between the researcher and the phenomena he is attempting to comprehend. Such barriers, from the vantage point of those employing a holistic analysis, inhibit and thwart the observer from an understanding of what is unique as well as what is generalizable from the data, and from perceiving the processes involved in contrast to simply the outcomes [Rist, 1977: 47].

A variety of proposed alternatives to the quantitative paradigm have been proposed. Some have suggested that a social systems model which focuses on the structural context within which social problems are approached is most appropriate (Etzioni, 1960; Schulberg and Baker, 1968; Suchman, 1970; and Ryan, 1971). The educational field provides a rich resource to new conceptual models which emphasize the social climate within which learning and other events are influenced and which in turn influence other organizational and interactional dimensions of the educational process (Smith and Brock, 1970; Center for New Schools, 1974; and Wilson, 1977). Other writers, as a result of these alternative conceptual frameworks, have emphasized specific aspects of the evaluation task which bear heavily on the process of conducting such assessments. For example, Krause and Howard (1976) highlight the political climate within which multiple publics have a say in how the evaluation question should be phrased, how the design of the research is planned and carried out, and how the feedback and utilization of these results can be enhanced. Both Guttentag (1973) and Scriven (1972) have discussed the role and meaning of subjectivity in the evaluation process while others, like Becker (1967) and Kourilsky (1973), have emphasized an adversary model.

Even among those individuals who have been prominently identified with the quantitative scientific model of evaluation, there are clear indications that such a framework has less relevance to effective evaluation efforts than the qualitative framework. For example, Campbell (1974: 200) has stated: "If qualitative and quantitative evaluations were to be organized on the same programs, I would expect them to agree. If they did not, I feel we should regard it possible that the quantitative was the one in error." In a similar vein, Cronbach (1975: 127) offers a telling commentary on how the means of the scientific method have become misguided ends in themselves.

The time has come to exorcise the null hypothesis. We cannot afford to pour costly data down the drain whenever effects present in a sample "fail to reach significance.". . . Let the author file descriptive information, at least in an archive, instead of reporting only those selected differences and correlations that are nominally "greater than chance." Descriptions encourage us to think constructively about results from quasi-replications, whereas the dichotomy significant/non-significant implies only a hopeless inconsistency. The canon of parsimony, misinterpreted, has lead to the habit of accepting Type II errors at every turn, for the sake of holding Type I errors in check. There are more things in heaven and earth than are dreamt of in our hypotheses, and our observations should be open to them.

WHAT QUALITATIVE METHODS CAN OFFER TO EVALUATION RESEARCH

Before proceeding with some suggestions regarding the role of qualitative methods in evaluation research, some words of caution are needed to prevent an overreaction to qualitative methods. Qualitative methods represent a legitimate research style. These methods, in their own right, can adequately evaluate an intervention program. They can even address the issue of causation. In addition, great advantages can be obtained in creatively combining qualitative and quantitative methods in evaluation research. What is inappropriate is to cast either method in an inferior position. Neither one has the corner on the "correct answers," although the quantitative method has gained a currency and credibility from its promoters and advocates that often border on fanaticism.

Each method reflects a stance toward the social world which embodies a unique perspective. According to Kuhn, each paradigm explains a limited amount of reality. So to some extent, the areas of a discipline's concerns are to a greater or lesser degree adequately covered by any given paradigm. In Kuhn's (1962: 18, 23) words,

> To be accepted as a paradigm, a theory must seem better than its competitors, but it need not, and in fact never does, explain all the facts with which it can be confronted. . . . paradigms gain their status because they are more successful than their competitors in solving a few problems that the group of practitioners have come to recognize as acute.

Shifts in paradigms occur because of the ascendance of anomalies, i.e., findings that are not expected under the given paradigm. If a discipline tries to explain these anomalies within the existing paradigm and fails, the work of normal science changes from one of "puzzle solving" to self-reflection and self-examination. Kuhn (1962: 90) states, "The proliferation of competing articulations, the willingness to try anything, the expression of explicit discontent, the recourse to philosophy and the debate over fundamentals, all these are symptoms of a transition from normal to extraordinary research."

The net result of this soul searching is a revolution—a revolution in the basic ways in which the discipline thinks about its phenomena, the assumptions that it takes for granted, the logic of its theory development, and the methodological principles that underlie its approach to the subject matter. Again, Kuhn (1970: 84-85) says it best:

> The transition from a paradigm in crisis to a new one from which a new tradition of normal science can emerge is far from a cumulative process, one achieved by an articulation or extension of the old paradigm. Rather, it is a reconstruction that changes some of the field's most elementary theoretical generalizations as well as many of its paradigm methods and applications. During the transition period there will be a large but never complete overlap between the problems that can be solved by the old and by the new paradigm. But there will also be a decisive difference in the modes of solution. When the transition is complete, the profession will have changed its view of the field, its methods, and its goals.

This is the present climate of evaluation research. While the pendulum is beginning to swing away from the quantitative evaluation model, it should not be allowed to swing too far toward the qualitatively focused evaluation. The middle ground of blending the assets of both approaches throughout an evaluation is optimal (Siedman, 1977; Trend, this volume) and will be illustrated in the following discussion.

Assume that a mental health care program needs to have an "empirical measure" of the program's effectiveness. The first step that could be taken is to talk with the program directors, selected staff, and selected patients (some who are starting treatment, some who are in treatment, some who are terminating treatment; also possibly some alumni) about what could be measures of effectiveness, how to actually "measure effectiveness," and so forth. Such a process would elicit the inputs of these publics, which can be incorporated in the design of the evaluation. Therefore, rule one suggests that the broadest base of information, including the meanings and implications of the evaluation, be used in assessments.

Following from this broad base of input, procedures need to be arranged to keep in contact with these publics during the course of the evaluation. This ongoing contact is critical to the process of keeping the evaluation close to the contextual worlds of those affected by it. At the same time, through the application of quantitative procedures one can attempt to expand the generalizability of the findings. For example, if symptom reduction were thought to be an appropriate measure of program impact, a questionnaire which had a history of use in other evaluation contexts might be chosen as a way not only to measure the concept but to consider the applicability of these data to other populations.

Throughout the evaluation process the concern should focus on tapping multiple perspectives and using multiple methods to capture the most comprehensive view of the social intervention. Therefore, "data triangulation" becomes an operational strategy (Denzin, 1970). Being able to arrive at similar conclusions about the program via different data sources enhances the validity of the observations made about a given aspect of the program.

The direction and course of the evaluation, although guided by the initial assumptions and suggestions gleaned in the process of defining the questions for evaluation, is corrected and modified based upon the impact of the ongoing evaluation and data collection. Therefore, the focus may change as the implications of the data being collected are identified.

Keeping track of the history of the evaluation also becomes an important task associated with the evaluation. Key events, changes in staffing, shifting purposes of the program, impacts of organizational constraints, and the significance of external events to the program's operation become benchmarks in a program's existence and need to be reviewed to detect their impact on the evaluation. This running record of the program's evolution becomes a source of stimulation for interviews and observations. Typically, key informants holding different perspectives or from various levels or positions within the organization can be very helpful in gaining an understanding of these events. For example, if symptom reduction were defined to be an objective of a program, it would be important to qualitatively identify the symptoms that patients and staff perceive as being reduced, the meanings of such events, and how such a condition affects and is affected by other events. If questionnaire measures of symptoms are planned, it would be helpful to ask patients what "things are bothering them most" and see if those events are identified by the symptom questionnaire. Establishing the face validity of the measures is necessary for the credibility of the findings and conclusions that may result from the evaluation. Therefore, the more one has multiple impact measures qualitatively understood and linked to quantitative measures from the key publics to an evaluation study, the greater the probability of understanding the impact and outcome of the intervention program.

It is quite common to obtain results which do not fit with what was expected. Engaging in speculation about rival explanations becomes frustrating because of the lack of contextual understanding which often surrounds the assessment. What could have "caused" such puzzling results? Was the instrument OK? Did the questions asked tap the area under study? Did the subjects perceive these questions in a different manner from what was anticipated? Did events occur internal or external to the social intervention program which could have affected the evaluation? The list of questions goes on and on. But the thrust of these questions is the same: Is there any qualitative data that can provide the framework for comprehending this evaluation within the larger context within which it occurred? Perhaps the bottom line in the integration of qualitative methods with quantitative methods in program evaluation activities is that the qualitative methods provide the context of meanings in which the quantitative findings can be understood.

Blumer (1969: 22) provides an insightful observation regarding the essential compatability of these two paradigms:

> The traditional position of idealism is that the "world of reality" exists only in human experience and that it appears only in the form in which human beings "see" the world. I think that this position is incontestable. It is impossible to cite a single instance of a characterization of the "world of reality" that is not cast in the form of human imagery. Nothing is known to human beings except in the form of something that they may indicate or refer to. To indicate anything, human beings must see it from their perspective; they must depict it as it appears to them. . . . However, this does not shift "reality," as so many conclude, from the empirical world to the realm of imagery and conception. . . . Such a solipsistic position is untenable because of the fact that the empirical world can "talk back" to our picture of it or assertions about it—talk back in the sense of challenging and resisting, or not bending to, our images or conceptions of it. This resistance gives the empirical world an obdurate character that is the mark of reality.

In short, qualitative methods provide a basis for understanding the substantive significance of the statistical associations that are found. This phenomenological basis for knowing is essential to the process of evaluating the impact of social intervention programs.

CONCLUSION

In summary, the increasing interest in qualitative methods in evaluation research stems from a dissatisfaction with the style of quantitative evaluations and a reconceptualization of the appropriateness of the scientific-quantitative model to the evaluation of intervention programs. Qualitative and quantitative methods are more than just differences between research strategies and data collection procedures. These approaches represent fundamentally different epistemological frameworks for conceptualizing the nature of knowing, social reality, and procedures for comprehending these phenomena. Qualitative methods are appropriate in their own right, as evaluation-assessment procedures of a program's impact. Program evaluation can be strengthened when both approaches are integrated into an evaluation design. Evaluation research, and the behavioral sciences in general, suffer from a preoccupation with quantification and statistics. A better balance needs to be struck between the everyday grounding of meanings in social action and the generalizability of these meanings to a wider context. This is the challenge offered by qualitative and quantitative methods. It is a challenge we can no longer ignore.

NOTE

1. Masterman (1970) offers a discussion of 21 different, but not mutually exclusive, ways in which Kuhn uses the term *paradigm*. She points out that three general notions are implied when Kuhn uses the term: "metaphysical paradigms" that provide organizing principles; "sociological paradigms" describing universally recognized achievements; and "construct paradigms" that describe methodological tools and instruments. For the most part, it appears that Kuhn means "metaphysical paradigms" when he uses the word.

REFERENCES

AIKEN, H. (1957) The Age of Ideology: The Nineteenth Century Philosophers. New York: George Braziller.
ATTKISSON, D. et al. (1978) Evaluation of Human Service Programs. New York: Academic Press.
BARNES, B. and S. SHAPIN (1979) Natural Order: Historical Studies of Scientific Culture. Beverly Hills: Sage.
BECKER, H. (1970) Sociological Work: Method and Substance. Chicago: Aldine.
——— (1967) "Whose side are we on?" Social Problems 14: 239-249.
——— and H. BARNES (1952) Social Thought From Lore to Science, Vols. 1 and 2. Washington, DC: Harren.
BLUMER, H. (1969) Symbolic Interactionism. Englewood Cliffs, NJ: Prentice-Hall.
BOGDAN, R. (1972) Participant Observation in Organizational Settings. Syracuse: Syracuse University Press.
——— and S. TAYLOR (1975) Introduction to Qualitative Research Methods. New York: John Wiley.
BRENNER, M., P. MARSH, and M. BRENNER [eds.] (1978) The Social Context of Method. London: Croom Helm.
BRITAN, G. (1978) "Experimental and contextual models of program evaluation." Evaluation and Program Planning 1: 229-234.
BRUYN, S. (1966) The Human Perspective. Englewood Cliffs, NJ: Prentice-Hall.
CAMPBELL, D. (1974) "Qualitative knowing in action research." Kurt Lewin Award Address, Society for the Psychological Study of Social Issues, meeting with the American Psychological Association, New Orleans, September 1. (to appear, after revision, in Journal of Social Issues.)
——— (1971) "Methods for the experimenting society." Presented at the American Psychological Association meeting, Washington, DC.
——— (1969) "Reforms as experiments." American Psychologist 24: 409-429.
——— and J. STANLEY (1966) Experimental and Quasi-Experimental Designs for Research. Chicago: Rand McNally.
CARO, F. (1971) Readings in Evaluation Research. New York: Russell Sage.
Center for New Schools (1974) The CNS Evaluation Model. Chicago: CNS. (mimeo)
COSER, L. (1971) Masters of Social Thought: Ideas in Historical and Social Context. New York: Harcourt Brace Jovanovich.

COURSEY, R. et al. (1977) Program Evaluation for Mental Health: Method, Strategies and Participants. New York: Grune and Stratton.

CRONBACH, L. (1975) "Beyond the two disciplines of scientific psychology." American Psychologist 30: 116-127.

DENZIN, N. (1970) The Research Act. Chicago: Aldine.

DOUGLAS, J. (1970) Understanding Everyday Life. Chicago: Aldine.

ERICKSON, F. (1977) "Some approaches to injury in school-community ethnography." Anthropology and Education Quarterly 8: 58-69.

ETZIONI, A. (1960) "Two approaches to organizational analysis: a critique and suggestion." Administrative Science Quarterly 5: 257-278.

FEYERABEND, P. (1975) Against Method: Outline of an Anarchistic Theory of Knowledge. London: Humanities Press.

FILSTEAD, W. (1978) Evaluating the Evaluations of Alcohol Programs. Ottawa, Canada: Non-Medical Use of Drugs, Directorate, National Health and Welfare.

——— (1976) "Sociological paradigms of reality," in H. R. Galvin (ed.) Phenomenology, Structuralism and Semiology. Lewisburg: Bucknell University Press.

——— (1975) "The promises and problems of qualitative methodology." Presented at the Social Science Symposium, Department of Sociology, American University.

——— (1973) "The natural history of a personal problem." Ph.D. Dissertation, Northwestern University.

——— [ed.] (1970) Qualitative Methodology: Firsthand Involvement with the Social World. Chicago: Markham.

GLASER, B. and A. STRAUSS (1967) The Discovery of Grounded Theory. Chicago: Aldine.

GLASER, E. (1969) A Qualitative Evaluation of the Concentrated Employment Program (CEP) in Birmingham, Detroit, Los Angeles, San Antonio, Seattle, and South Bronx, by Means of the Participant Observation Method. Final Report to the Office of Evaluation, Manpower Administration, U.S. Department of Labor. Los Angeles: Human Interaction Research Institute.

GUTTENTAG, M. (1973) "Subjectivity and its use in evaluation research." Evaluation 1: 60-65.

HABERMAN, J. (1971) Knowledge and Human Interests. Boston: Beacon.

HAMILTON, D. et al. (1977) Beyond the Numbers Game: A Reader in Educational Evaluation. Berkeley: McCutchan.

JUNKER, G. (1960) Field Work: An Introduction to the Social Sciences. Chicago: University of Chicago Press.

KOURILSKY, M. (1973) "An adversary model for educational evaluation." Education Comment 3: 3-6.

KRAUSE, M. and K. HOWARD (1976) "Program evaluation in the public interest: a new research methodology." Community Mental Health Journal 12: 291-300.

KUHN, T. (1970) The Structure of Scientific Revolutions. Chicago: University of Chicago Press.

——— (1962) The Structure of Scientific Revolutions. Chicago: Phoenix.

LOFLAND, J. (1976) Doing Social Life. New York: John Wiley.

——— (1973) Analyzing Social Settings. Belmont: Wadsworth.

MASTERMAN, M. (1970) "The nature of a paradigm," in I. Lasotos and M. Musgrave (eds.) Criticism and Growth of Knowledge. Cambridge: Cambridge University Press.

McCALL, G. and J. SIMMONS [eds.] (1969) Issues in Participant Observation. Reading, MA: Addison-Wesley.

MECH, E. (1969) Participant Observation: Toward An Evaluative Methodology for Manpower Programs. Final Report to the Office of Evaluation, Manpower Administration, U.S. Department of Labor. Tempe: Arizona State University.

MITROFF, I. (1974) The Subjective Side of Science: A Philosophical Inquiry into the Psychology of Apollo Moon Scientists. Amsterdam: Elsever.

PATTON, M. (1978) Utilization-Focused Evaluation. Beverly Hills: Sage.

——— (1975) Alternative Evaluation Research Paradigm. Grand Forks: University of North Dakota Press.

POLANYI, M. (1958) Personal Knowledge. London: Routledge and Kegan Paul.

POPPER, K. (1972) Objective Knowledge: An Evolutionary Approach. Oxford: Clarendon Press.

QUINE, W. (1969) Ontological Relativity. New York: Columbia University Press.

RIECKEN, H. and R. F. BORUCH [eds.] (1974) Social Experimentation: A Method For Planning and Evaluating Social Interventions. New York: Academic Press.

RIST, R. (1977) "On the relations among educational research paradigms: from disdain to detente." Anthropology and Education Quarterly 8: 42-49.

ROSSI, P. and H. WILLIAMS (1972) Evaluating Social Programs: Theory, Practice and Politics. New York: Seminar Press.

RYAN, W. (1971) Blaming the Victims. New York: Pantheon.

SCHULBERG, H. and F. BAKER (1968) "Program evaluation models and the implementation of research findings." American Journal of Public Health 58: 1248-1255.

SCHUTZ, A. (1967) The Phenomenology of the Social World. Evanston: Northwestern University Press.

SCWARTZ, H. and J. JACOBS (1979) Qualitative Sociology. New York: Free Press.

SCRIVEN, M. (1972) "Objectivity and subjectivity in educational research," in H. B. Dunkel et al. (eds.) Philosophical Redirectory of Educational Research. Chicago: National Society for the Study of Education.

SIEDMAN, E. (1977) "Why not qualitative analysis." Public Administration Review 37: 415-417.

SJOBERG, G. and R. NETT (1966) A Methodology for Social Research. New York: Harper & Row.

SMITH, L. and J. BROCK (1970) Go Bug Go! Methodological Issues in Classroom Observational Research." Occasional Paper Series: No. 5. St. Ann, Missouri: Central Midwestern Regional Educational Laboratory.

SOBEL, L. (1976) "An assessment of the use of qualitative social science methods in program evaluation research." Seattle: University of Washington. (unpublished)

STRUENING, E. and M. GUTTENTAG [eds.] (1975) Handbook of Evaluation Research, Vols. 1 and 2. Beverly Hills: Sage.

SUCHMAN, E. (1970) "Action for what? critique of evaluative research," in R. O'Toole (ed.) The Organization, Management, and Tactics of Social Research. Cambridge: Schennan.

TIKUNOFF, W. and B. WARD [ed.] (1977) "Exploring qualitative/quantitative research methodologies in education." Anthropology and Educational Quarterly 8: 37-163.

WEISS, R. and M. REIN (1972) "The evaluation of broad aim programs: difficulties in experimental design and alternatives," in C. Weiss (ed.) Evaluating Action Programs. Boston: Allyn & Bacon.

WILSON, S. (1977) "The use of ethnographic techniques in educational research." Review of Educational Research 47: 245-265.

Donald T. Campbell

Syracuse University

3

"DEGREES OF FREEDOM" AND THE CASE STUDY

Quantitative vs. qualitative methodology. A controversy between "qualitative" vs. "quantitative" modes of knowing, between *geiteswissenchaftlich* and *naturwissenschaftlich* approaches, between "humanistic" and "scientific" approaches is characterstic of most of the social sciences in the U.S.A. today. In fields such as sociology and social psychology, many of our ablest and most dedicated graduate students are increasingly opting for the qualitative, humanistic mode. In political science, there has been a continuous division along these lines. Only economics and geography seem relatively immune.

Inevitably, this split has spilled over into evaluation research, taking the form of a controversy over the legitimacy of the quantitative-experimental paradigm for program evaluation (e.g., Weiss & Rein, 1969, 1970; Guttentag, 1971, 1973; Campbell, 1970; Salasin, 1973). The issue has not, to be sure, been argued in quite these terms. The critics taking what I am calling the humanistic position are often well-trained in quantitative-experimental methods. Their specific criticisms are often well-grounded in the experimentalist's own framework: experiments implementing a single treatment

AUTHOR'S NOTE: *The beginning section of this article entitled "Quantitative vs. qualitative methodology" is reprinted (with minor editorial revision) from "Assessing the Impact of Planned Social Change" in G. M. Lyons [ed.] (1975) from* Social Research and Public Policies, *Hanover, New Hampshire: University Press of New England. A version of that full paper was presented to the Visegard, Hungary, Conference on Social Psychology, May 5-10, 1974. Preparation of that paper was supported in part by grants from the Russell Sage Foundation and the National Science Foundation, Grant SOC-7103704-03. The remainder of the article is reprinted (with minor editorial change) from "Degrees of Freedom and the Case Study,"* Comparative Political Studies, *1975, 8: 178:193. That paper was based on a presentation to the SSRC Workshop on Comparative Methodology meeting at Harvard University, August 1970. Its preparation in that form was supported by NSF Grant SOC-7103704-03.*

in a single setting are profoundly ambiguous as to what caused what; there is a precarious rigidity in the measurement system, limiting recorded outcomes to those dimensions anticipated in advance; process is often neglected in an experimental program focused on the overall effect of a complex treatment, and thus knowing such effects has only equivocal implications for program replication or improvement; broad-gauge programs are often hopelessly ambiguous as to goals and relevant indicators; changes of treatment program during the course of an ameliorative experiment, while practically essential, make input-output experimental comparisons uninterpretable; social programs are often implemented in ways that are poor from an experimental design point of view; even under well-controlled situations, experimentation is a profoundly tedious and equivocal process; experimentation is too slow to be politically useful; etc. All these are true enough, often enough, to motivate a vigorous search for alternatives. So far, the qualitative-knowing alternatives suggested (e.g., Weiss & Rein, 1969, 1970; Guttentag, 1971, 1973) have not been persuasive to me. Indeed, I believe that naturalistic observation of events is an intrinsically equivocal arena for causal inference, by qualitative or quantitative means, because of the ubiquitous confounding of selection and treatment. Any efforts to reduce that equivocality will have the effect of making conditions more "experimental." "Experiments" are, in fact, just that type of contrived observational setting optimal for causal inference. The problems of inference surrounding program evaluation are intrinsic to program settings in ongoing social processes. Experimental designs do not cause these problems, and, in fact, alleviate them, though often only slightly so.

In such protests, there often seems implicitly a plea for the substitution of qualitative clairvoyance for the indirect and presumptive processes of science. But while I must reject this aspect of the humanistic protest, there are other aspects of it that have motivated these critics in which I can wholeheartedly join. These other criticisms may be entitled "neglect of relevant qualitative contextual evidence" or "overdependence upon a few quantified abstractions to the neglect of contradictory and supplementary qualitative evidence."

Too often quantitative social scientists, under the influence of missionaries from logical positivism, presume that in true science, quantitative knowing replaces qualitative, common-sense knowing. The situation is in fact quite different. Rather, science depends upon qualitative, common-sense knowing even though at best it goes beyond it. Science in the end contradicts some items of common sense, but it only does so by trusting the great bulk of the rest of common-sense knowledge. Such revision of common sense by science is akin to the revision of common sense by common sense which, paradoxically, can only be done by trusting more common sense. Let us consider as an example the Muller-Lyer illustration (Figure 1).

If you ask the normal resident of a "carpentered" culture (Segall, et al., 1966) which line is longer, *a* or *b*, he will reply *b*. If you supply him with a ruler, or allow him to use the edge of another piece of paper as a makeshift ruler, he will eventually convince himself that he is wrong, and that line *a* is longer. In so deciding he will have rejected as inaccurate one product of visual perception by trusting a larger set of other visual perceptions. He will also have made many presumptions, inexplicit for the most part, including the assumption that the lengths of the lines have remained relatively constant during the measurement process, that the ruler was rigid rather than elastic, that the heat and moisture of his hand have not changed the ruler's length in such a coincidental way as to produce the different measurements, expanding it when approaching line *b* and contracting it when approaching line *a*, etc.

Let us take as another example a scientific paper containing theory and experimental results demonstrating the particulate nature of light, in dramatic contrast to common-sense understanding. Or a scientific paper demonstrating that what ordinary perception deems "solids" are in fact open lattices. Were such a paper to limit itself to mathematical symbols and purely scientific terms, omitting ordinary language, it would fail to communicate to another scientist in such a way as to enable him to replicate the experiment and verify the observations. Instead, the few scientific terms have been imbedded in a discourse of elliptical prescientific ordinary language which the reader is presumed to (and presumes to) understand. And in the laboratory work of the original and replicating laboratory, a common-sense, prescientific language and perception of objects, solids, and light was employed and trusted in coming to the conclusions that thus

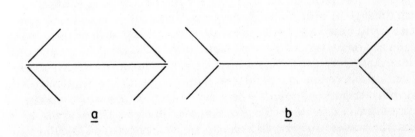

a   b

Figure 1.

revise the ordinary understanding. To challenge and correct the common-sense understanding in one detail, common-sense understanding in general had to be trusted.

Related to this is the epistemological emphasis on qualitative-pattern identification as prior to an identification of quantifiable atomic particles, in reverse of the logical atomist's intuition, still too widespread (Campbell, 1966). Such an epistemology is fallibilist, rather than clairvoyant, emphasizing the presumptive error-proneness of such pattern identification, rather than perception as a dependable ground of certainty. But it also recognizes this fallible, intuitive, presumptive, ordinary perception to be the only route. This is not to make perceptions uncriticizable (Campbell, 1969), but they are, as we have seen, only criticizable by trusting many other perceptions of the same epistemic level.

If we apply such an epistemology to evaluation research, it immediately legitimizes the "narrative history" portion of most reports and suggests that this activity be given formal recognition in the planning and execution of the study, rather than only receiving attention as an afterthought. Evaluation studies are uninterpretable without this, and most would be better interpreted with more. That this content is subjective and guilty of perspectival biases should lead us to better select those who are invited to record the events, and to prepare formal procedures whereby all interested participants can offer additions and corrections to the official story. The use of professionally trained historians, anthropologists, and qualitative sociologists should be considered. The narrative history is an indispensable part of the final report, and the best qualitative methods should be used in preparing it.

We should also recognize that participants and observers have been evaluating program innovations for centuries without benefit of quantification or scientific method. This is the common-sense knowing which our scientific evidence should build upon and go beyond, not replace. But it is usually neglected in quantitative evaluations, unless a few supporting anecdotes haphazardly collected are included. Under the epistemology I advocate, one should attempt to systematically tap all the qualitative common-sense program critiques and evaluations that have been generated among the program staff, program clients and their families, and community observers. While quantitative procedures such as questionnaires and rating scales will often be introduced at this stage for reasons of convenience in collecting and summarizing, non-quantitative methods of collection and compiling should also be considered, such as hierarchically organized discussion groups. Where such evaluations are contrary to the quantitative results, the quantitative results should be regarded as suspect until the reasons for the discrepancy are well understood. Neither is infallible, of course. But for many of us, what needs to be emphasized is that the quantitative results may be as mistaken as the qualitative. After all, in physical science laboratories, the meters often work improperly, and it is usually qualitative knowing, plus assumptions about what the meter ought to be showing, that discovers the malfunction. (This is a far cry from the myth that meter readings operationally define theoretical parameters.)

It is with regret that I report that in U.S. program evaluations, this sensible joint use of modes of knowing is not yet practiced. Instead, there seems to be an all-or-none flip-flop. Where, as in Model Cities evaluations, anthropologists have been used as observers, this has often been in place of, rather than in addition to, quantitative indicators, pretests, posttests, and control-group comparisons. A current example of the use of anthropologists is the "Experimental Schools" program started in the U.S. Office of Education and now in the National Institute of Education. In this program, school-system initiative is encouraged, and winning programs receive substantial increments to their budgets (say 25%) for use in implementing the innovations. To evaluate some of these programs, very expensive contracts have been let for anthropological process evaluations of single programs. In one case, this was to involve a team of five anthropologists for five years, studying the school system for a unique city with a population of 100,000 persons. The anthropologists have had no prior experience with any other U.S. school system. They have been allowed no base-line period of study before the program was introduced, they arrived instead after the program had started. They were not scheduled to study any other comparable school system not undergoing this change. To believe that under these disadvantaged observational conditions, these qualitative observers could infer what aspects of the processes they observe were due to the new program innovation requires more faith than I have, although I should withhold judgment until I see the products. Furthermore, the emphasis of the study is on the primary observations of the anthropologists themselves, rather than on their role in using participants as informants. As a result there is apt to be a neglect of the observations of other qualitative observers better placed than the anthropologists. These include the parents who have had other children in the school prior to the change; the teachers who have observed this one system before, during, and after the change; the teachers who have transferred in with prior experience in otherwise comparable systems; and the students themselves. Such observations one would perhaps want to mass produce in the form of questionnaires. If so, one would wish that appropriate questions had also been asked prior to the experimental program, and on both occasions in some comparable school system undergoing no such reform, thus reestablishing experimental design and quantitative summaries of qualitative judgments. (For a more extended discussion of the qualitative-quantitative issues, see Campbell, 1974.)

THE CASE STUDY

The dominant mode of study in anthropology, comparative political science, and comparative sociology remains the intensive study of a single foreign setting by an outsider for whom this is the only intensively experienced foreign culture. Such studies may be written by "trained" social scientists or by "amateur" observers (such as missionaries, diplomats, newspaper reporters, businessmen, soldiers of fortune, or tourists) whose observations and leisure may provoke them to write on the foreign-to-them culture. Even when these amateur observers do not write, they participate strongly in enculturating the social scientist into the foreign culture, or into the expatriate accommodation to that culture (Kidder, 1971). Another similar genre is descriptions of one's own country done while or after being a resident in another, as Kenyatta (1938) describing the Kikuyu while in England as a student of Malinowski. Such knowing, written or unwritten, I will use to represent "common-sense knowing" for comparative social science. If we achieve a meaningful quantitative 100-nation correlation, it is by dependence on this kind of knowing at every point, not by replacing it with a "scientific" quantitative methodology which substitutes for such knowing. The quantitative multination generalization will contradict such anecdotal, single-case, naturalistic observation at some points, but it will do so only by trusting a much larger body of such anecdotal, single-case, naturalistic observations.

This is not to say that such common-sense naturalistic observation is objective, dependable, or unbiased. But it is all that we have. It is the only route to knowledge—noisy, fallible, and biased though it be. We should be aware of its weaknesses, but must still be willing to trust it if we are to go about the process of comparative (or monocultural) social science at all. I will come back to the biases later, but first, let me try to correct some of my own prior excesses in describing the case study approach. The caricature of the single case study approach which I have had in mind consists of an observer who notes a single striking characteristic of a culture, and then has available all of the other differences on all other variables to search through in finding an explanation. He may have very nearly all of the causal concepts in his language on which to draw. That he will find an "explanation" that seems to fit perfectly becomes inevitable, through his total lack of "degrees of freedom." (It is as though he were trying to fit two points of observation with a formula including a thousand adjustable terms, whereas in good science, we must have fewer terms in our formula than our data points.)

This orientation was expressed in Campbell and Stanley (1966: 6, 7) as follows (a legitimate citation since many have noted cross-cultural comparisons as a weak form of quasi-experimental design; e.g., Lijphart, 1971: 683-685; Boesch and Eckensberger, 1969):

Pre-Experimental Designs
1. The One-Shot Case Study

Much research . . . today conforms to a design in which a single group is studied only once, subsequent to some agent or treatment presumed to cause change. Such studies might be diagramed as follows:

$$X \quad 0$$

As has been pointed out (e.g., Boring, 1954; Stouffer, 1949) such studies have such a total absence of control as to be of almost no scientific value. The design is introduced here as a minimum reference point. Yet because of the continued investment in such studies and the drawing of causal inferences from them, some comment is required. Basic to scientific evidence (and to all knowledge-diagnostic processes including the retina of the eye) is the process of comparison, or recording differences, or of contrast. Any appearance of absolute knowledge, or intrinsic knowledge about singular isolated objects, is found to be illusory upon analysis. Securing scientific evidence involves making at least one comparison. For such a comparison to be useful, both sides of the comparison should be made with similar care and precision.

In the case studies of Design 1, a carefully studied single instance is implicitly compared with other events casually observed and remembered. The inferences are based upon general expectations of what the data would have been had the X not occurred, etc. Such studies often involve tedious collection of specific detail, careful observation, testing, and the like, and in such instances involve the error of *misplaced precision*. How much more valuable the study would be if the one set of observations were reduced by half and the saved effort directed to the study in equal detail of an appropriate comparison instance. It seems well-nigh unethical at the present time to allow, as theses or dissertations in education, case studies of this nature (i.e., involving a single group observed at one time only). "Standardized" tests in such case studies provide only very limited help, since the rival sources of difference other than X are so numerous as to render the "standard" reference group almost useless as a "control group." On the same grounds, the many uncontrolled sources of difference between a present case study and potential future ones which might be compared with it are so numerous as to make justification in terms of providing a bench mark for future studies also hopeless. In general, it would be better to apportion the descriptive effort between both sides of an interesting comparison.

My strong rejection of the single case study, or indeed, of a two-site comparison, was also expressed in my chapter in Hsu's (1961) book as follows:

> *The uninterpretability of comparisons between but two natural instances.* In view of the importance of Malinowski's challenge to the love-jealousy interpretation of the Oedipal conflict, it is unforgivable that his observations have not been replicated. However thorough his field work on other points, his published evidence on this point is very thin indeed. While he alludes to evidence from manifest dream content, what we need are substantial samples of detailed records of the dreams of boys and girls and men and women.
>
> But while there is a crying need for verifying and extending Malinowski's evidence of Trobriand intrafamilial attitudes, such a replication is of minor importance for testing the Freudian hypothesis. We who are interested in using such data for delineating process rather than exhaustively describing single instances must accept this rule:
>
> *No comparison of a single pair of natural objects is interpretable.* Between Trobriand and Vienna there are many dimensions of differences which could constitute potential rival explanations and which we have no means of ruling out. For comparisons of this pair, the *ceteris paribus* requirement becomes untenable. But data collection need not stop here. Both the avunculate and the European arrangement are so widely distributed over the world that if testing Oedipal theories were our purpose, we could select a dozen matched pairs of tribes from widely varying culture areas, each pair differing with regard to which male educates and disciplines the boy, but as similar as possible in other respects. Assuming that collections of dreams from boys showed the expected differences between each pair, then the more such pairs we had, the fewer tenable rival hypotheses would be available and, thus, the more certain would be our confirmation [Campbell, 1961: 344-345].

A third presentation:

> Seen in this light, the problem of the "laboratory" of actual international relations is that there are too few actors, too few occasions, too few "reruns" in which sets of actors, classifiable as comparable, start interacting from comparable starting points, and far too many obviously relevant theoretical considerations. The degrees of freedom for *post*dictions, for testing the theory on the body of data that suggested it, are much fewer than for *pre*-dictions (an aspect of this feature is enshrined in the one-tailed vs. two-tailed test-of-significance distinction). These problems are as real and as defeating for the qualitative essays of the knowledgeable political scientist or historian as for the multivariate statistician. Communicating the problem to the latter may be easier (though often difficult enough when he claims to be describing a total universe) because the latter has made explicit the number of variables, while the scholar has an unexplicit but very large number of potential "considerations" which he has, or could have, brought to bear on one instance or

another. (This, rather than its pattern-recognition characteristics, is the crux of the problems of the *Verstehen* approach—one source of its exquisitely satisfactory fit to particular instances, and its unsatisfactoriness as a reality-testing process.) [Raser et al., 1970: 186-187].

While it is probable that many case studies professing or implying interpretation or explanation, or relating the case to theory, are guilty of these faults, it now seems to me clear that not all are, or need be, and that I have overlooked a major source of discipline (i.e., of degrees of freedom if I persist in using this statistical concept for the analogous problem in non-statistical settings). In a case study done by an alert social scientist who has thorough local acquaintance, the theory he uses to explain the focal difference also generates predictions or expectations on dozens of other aspects of the culture, and he does not retain the theory unless most of these are also confirmed. In some sense, he has tested the theory with degrees of freedom coming from the multiple implications of any one theory. The process is a kind of pattern-matching (Campbell, 1966; Raser, 1969) in which there are many aspects of the pattern demanded by theory that are available for matching with his observations on the local setting.

Experiences of social scientists confirm this. Even in a single qualitative case study the conscientious social scientist often finds no explanation that seems satisfactory. Such an outcome would be impossible if the caricature of the single case study as presented in these three quotations were correct—there would instead be a surfeit of subjectively compelling explanations. While I have no doubt that there is a statistically significant bias in favor of drawing conclusions rather than holding belief in abeyance in the face of essentially random evidence (Campbell, 1959; demonstrated for animals by Tolman and Krechevsky, 1933; and by B. F. Skinner's research on superstition in pigeons), this cannot be a dominant bias, as both biological and social evolution would have eliminated such credulity in favor of more discriminating mutants. That is, our common-sense mechanisms of knowing must have had a net adaptive value, at least for the ecology in which they were evolved.

Becker (personal communication; see also Becker, 1970: 39-62, 25-38) assures me that almost invariably the social scientist undertaking an intensive case study, by means of participant observation and other qualitative common-sense approaches to acquaintance, ends up finding out that his prior beliefs and theories were wrong. If so, this is an important fact, and one worth systematic documentation. If so, it shows that the intensive cross-cultural case study has a discipline and a capacity to reject theories which are neglected in my caricature of the method.

Naroll (1962), one of the arch quantifiers of anthropology, acquires a powerful tool for data quality control in quantitative studies from classifying the "quality" of the ethnographer. It is noteworthy that the criteria of quality come not from the use by the ethnographer of any special tool of quantitative social science (such as random sampling procedures, structured interview schedules, psychological tests, and so forth), but rather from superior qualitative acquaintance with the culture described, for example, through longer residence and better knowledge of the local language.

Perhaps it will help to illustrate the principle of discipline and degrees of freedom from multiple theoretical implications to report some first-hand observations on the early stages of a famous case study. In the fall of 1940 at Berkeley, I was a student in a seminar on culture and personality led by A. L. Kroeber and E. H. Erickson and devoted to the Yurok Indians of Northern California among whom Erikson had just been studying. From these materials, Erikson eventually produced his classic "Observations of the Yurok" (1943). Kroeber had studied these people some twenty or so years earlier and had encouraged Erikson to study them. Kroeber had taken Erikson up to the Yurok and had introduced him to his surviving friends and informants of twenty years earlier. Appropriately enough, Kroeber opened the seminar with a description of the Yurok, a description which included not only their geographical situation, economy, culture area membership, social organization, physical artifacts, and so on, but also the statement that they were classic embodiments of the Freudian anal character structure. I remember him epitomizing this structure, and the Yurok, with a long alliteration of adjectives beginning with "p," possibly something like "parsimonious, pedantic, prudish, petulant, paranoid," though the details escape me. In any event, Kroeber set the stage for an orthodox, confirmatory exercise in psychoanalytic anthropology. Kroeber had been analyzed and had practiced psychoanalysis for several years, 1918-1922, in San Francisco (T. Kroeber, 1970). His loyalties to anthropological factuality were clearly stronger than his loyalties to Freudian theory, as evidenced in his famous reviews of *Totem and Taboo* (Kroeber, 1920, 1939), but on this occasion his orientation was orthodox Freudian. Undoubtedly, he had encouraged Erikson to visit the Yurok in the belief that they were an ideal type in Freudian culture-character typology.

Erikson was at that time a thoroughly orthodox Freudian. He had done a psychoanalytic ethnography of the Sioux (1939) whose prolonged breast feeding, with its concomitant prohibitions against biting mother's breast, led to a compensatory oral-dental fixation, exhibited in biting humor and in nervous habits of biting sticks, straws, and fingernails. He had creatively advanced the Freudian theory of child development with his elaborate typology of modes and zones of libidinal fixation in childhood (1950: 44-92), but this was in an orthodox, albeit novel, elaboration. If the qualitative case study of a single cultural setting were as devoid of discipline of degrees of freedom as my caricatures had it, surely in this case an orthodox Freudian anal syndrome would have been confirmed. But it was not.

Erikson could find nothing in the present or past toilet training of children that would have produced an anal fixation of any type. This provides a dramatic instance of a *theory-infirming case study,* in the terms of Lijphart's (1971) fine analysis, but one with considerably more disproving impact than he allows for, since he too neglects the discipline coming from a richness of relevant details.

Not only did Erikson abandon, for the Yurok at least, the anal character hypothesis, he generated another hypothesis and tested it on the Yurok data. Of the innumerable alternative solutions that occurred to him to solve the puzzles of the data, *most were untenable for one reason or another.* I emphasize this phrase because it seems to epitomize the use of multiple implications, multiple observations ("for one reason or another") in a conceptual population, a population of the multiple implications of any one specific theory: degrees of freedom from multiple implications. The one theory he ended up retaining was corroborated by multiple diverse observations of the very sort that had weeded out his other trial solutions. I do not have space here to convey convincingly his solution, and its initial implausibility is made worse in the following oversimplification: rather than an oral or an anal fixation, the Yurok were fixated on the whole alimentary canal. This thesis organized a great wealth of the unusual features of the culture, such as their preoccupation with the Klamath River which flowed into and out of their small valley, their sweat houses with separate entrances and exits, their teaching tales for children, including the hummingbird who flew in the mouth and out the anus of a bear, and so on. Reading the original monograph is much more convincing. (My own seminar paper, done jointly with Frederick M. Geier, was an effort to make psychological sense of a collection of thirty or forty Yurok myths by projective test methods. Erikson's new theory was not, as I remember, available to us during the seminar. The effort was so frustrating that we regressed to undergraduate humor and put a leitmotif on the title page, attributed to Confucius: "One speaks verily of myth-interpretation only if one lispeth.")

This disciplining aspect of conscientious, sensitive, self-critical case studies, which I have tried to relate here to the statistical concept of having sufficient degrees of freedom to test the fit of hypotheses, is no doubt an aspect of the principles of pattern-matching and context-dependence (Campbell, 1966). Also, I am probably making, belatedly, the same argument as have Lasswell (1968) and others (e.g., Raser, 1969) in insisting on a configurational approach. A thorough epistemological-statistical analysis of the situation is yet to be done. This partial recanting is but a beginning, and in order to reopen the problem I am probably presenting here an exaggerated defense. For certainly the theoretical mind is capable of remarkably flexible post hoc rationalization of any outcome, and in such rationalizations, overinterpretation, capitalization on chance, and exhaustion of degrees of freedom do often occur. For an example in Erikson's problem area, one can look to the contrast between Kardiner's (1939) presentation of Du Bois's material on Alor and her own presentation (1944). To buttress his oral deprivation theme, Kardiner gives great attention to one child who, given an eared balloon to play with, tried to suck one of the balloon's ears and was photographed so doing. He neglects more relevant contra-indicants including the absence of thumb-sucking. In general, where a careful, quantitative study fails to confirm a widely held belief, one will usually trust most the quantitative study. But this, in turn, has rejected the one common-sense belief only by depending on a host of others. Ordinary social knowing, of course, is subject to many specific biases, some I shall now go into. But it remains the only route. Even when we improve on it, we must go through it and build on it.

The testimony from Becker and the case of Erikson go against a well-known general bias in favor of finding things as one expects them to be. Francis Bacon ensconced it as the first of the "Idols [false images] of the Tribe." "The human understanding, from its peculiar nature, easily supposes a greater degree of order and equality in things than it really finds. When any proposition has been laid down, the human understanding forces everything else to add fresh support and confirmation. It is the peculiar and perpetual error of the human understanding to be more moved and excited by affirmatives than negatives" (Bacon, 1853: the quotation is from the Aphorisms, Bk. 1, XLVI). For perceptual judgments of out-of-focus pictures, I have participated in one clear confirmation of it (Wyatt and Campbell, 1951) and many others exist in the literature (reviewed by Campbell, 1959). But while universal to some degree, it is still a marginal bias. In our experiment, the bias reduced by 15% or so the accuracy that would have been present without the expectation and disappeared as the pictures were brought into clear focus (Wyatt and Campbell, 1951). This is, of course, a bias which physical perception and social perception share. It is often in conflict with a bias related to fluctuating adaptation levels (Helson, 1964) that cause an observer to notice novel contrasts at the expense of sameness (Campbell, 1961: 341-344; 1959).

Since single-culture case studies will continue to be the major form of comparative social science, it may be well to offer a few suggestions for improving the discipline such studies offer as probes for theory. These suggestions are based on analogues from quantitative studies. Quantitative studies, as published, are not by any means immune from these problems, as we shall see. But quantitative studies lead to efforts to set significance levels which in turn lead to awareness of subtle aspects of the problem. In what follows, the major general recommendation is that the researcher doing a single-site case study keep more explicit records on the analogous aspects of his problem-solving activities.

The best known problem regarding degrees of freedom in tests of significance is the number of observations against which the hypothesis is checked. For similar replications within a culture site, the fieldworker is usually already alert to this, e.g., the number of observed villages in which the leadership pattern holds and the number in which it does not. What is here being suggested is that an analogous record be kept for the box score of implications of the theory, aspiring to a full record of all of the theory-testing thoughts and investigations that take this form: If theory A is true, then B, C, and D ought to follow. Where these implications have motivated him to active search, recording will be easy. Where the test has been adequately completed in the thought process alone, much of the implication count will be lost. But even for these thought trials, a self-conscious attention to the problem can result in much more complete recording than case study monographs now present. Much of this puzzle-worrying is no doubt literally unconscious and/or during sleep, as Poincare argues (1913). Thus a full record will not be achieved. Probably the most common omission would be the neglect of implications that do not fit, particularly by the more theory-driven observers. The cumulative literature of other studies and of criticism provides a slow and partial curb to this. We need a tradition of deliberately fostering an adversary process in which other experts are encouraged to look for other implications of the theory and other facts to contradict or support it. Some of this is now done, but not in a form that would generate a box score of hits and misses. A further curb on the inevitable residual ethnocentrism of social scientists would be a practice of inviting local social scientists to present dissenting and affirming footnotes and commentaries along with the original publication of the regional monographs. This would also help to expand the box scores of hits and misses. For almost every classic theory-relevant case study there are as yet unused predictions on which to cross-validate them. (Perhaps the Yurok myths Geier and I worked would provide such an arena for Erikson's hypothesis.) If it is an important study, it is worth a confirmatory case study.

A second degrees-of-freedom, test-of-significance issue worth borrowing is the distinction between one-tailed and two-tailed tests. This can perhaps be translated into the case study setting as a distinction between the confirmatory value of an agreement between implication and facts when the theory has been chosen in light of those facts versus the higher confirmatory value when the theory has been chosen without knowledge of these confirmations. Certainly, the box score should keep these two types separate. Moreover, when the theory correctly predicts a fact that would be very unexpected from the point of view of common sense or other theories or other cultures, for example, the confirmation is correctly a lot more convincing than when the prediction is banal. This point is not easily recognized in the tests-of-significance tradition (Meehl, 1967), but is in the history of science as in Galileo's use of the phases of the moons of Jupiter. A Bayesian orientation could probably be used to focus on comparison of prior probabilities, given theory A, as opposed to the prior probabilities given other theories. This does not seem typical of Bayesian applications, which are more apt to treat for one theory at a time the prior probabilities and the probabilities after data collection. However this may be, one can certainly recommend the attention of a Bayesian statistician-epistemologist to the theory-testing case study problem. This problem should also be elaborated separately for each one of Lijphart's (1971) six types of case study (e.g., hypothesis-generating, theory-confirming, theory-infirming, and so forth) with particular attention to the difference in the degrees of freedom when one has chosen, for example, the site expecting it to be confirmatory after an implicit or explicit search of many cultures for such an instance, versus going in blind and happening on a confirmation. Prior knowledge of extremity on one of two variables of relevance, or on both, or on neither, all affect the problem of degrees of freedom, i.e., of capitalization on chance. Lijphart's analysis is very relevant here, although he, like my earlier presentations, neglects testing from multiple implications with a single case.

A final degrees-of-freedom problem is not yet well represented in published statistical studies, but is of increasing concern. This is the issue of doing tests of multiple hypotheses and then writing up as conclusions those that are "statistically significant" by a significance test which assumes that one went into the inquiry with only this one hypothesis. Thus if one's data had been generated in fact solely from random numbers, if one studies all of the interrelationships among 15 variables, generating 105 hypothesized two-variable relationships, $1/20$ of these or 5+ would be found "significant" at the 5% level. The problem emerges in the literature as the "error rate experiment-wise" (Ryan, 1960) and the "problem of multiple comparisons" Scheffé, 1953) or of "data dredging" (Selvin and Stuart, 1966). Combined with the problem of number of observations, it can be noted in a form particularly acute for political science studies correlating dimensions of nations: If one has as many variables as nations, then the multiple correlation relating any one variable to the others will be 1.00, even if all data are random numbers. (This can be seen from the "shrinkage" formula for R; Lord and Novick, 1968: 286). The R's computed on small samples are regularly smaller when cross-validated on new samples. This formula estimates such shrinkage in the absence of cross-validation. In factor analytic studies, it emerges as the truism that with smaller samples of nations, larger factor loadings and more factors will be found due to the greater sampling variability of correlation coefficients with small n's. This is the proper explanation of the recurrent finding that factor structures are clearer and explain more when data are analyzed by continents rather than pooled for the whole world.

To handle this problem in the hypothesis-generating case study, such as the second phase of Erikson's work on the Yurok, one should keep a record of all of the theories considered in the creative puzzle-solving process. To represent the degrees of freedom from multiple implications, one should also keep a record of the implications against which each was tested, and the box score of hits and misses. I am personally convinced that Erikson's alimentary canal theory is better than the pseudo-perfect multiple correlation arising from exhausting one's degrees of freedom by testing too many hypotheses on too few cases or implications. I am also convinced that case studies can be improved in their theory-testing value in this regard. When one also recognizes the reality of higher-order interaction among variables (e.g., the relation of variables A and B being different for different levels of C, D, E, and so on), one must recognize that the plethora of plausible hypotheses and the fewness or costliness of instances create real limits for a comparative social science. But the recognition of instances in implication-space, to supplement the instances of persons, villages, nations, eras, and so on, alleviates the problem at least a little.

One more suggestion for improving the case study is offered. The single case study, as presented above, is in reality a comparison of two cases: the original culture and the foreign culture. But this is a very asymmetrical comparison, asymmetrical on a number of important parameters: one culture is learned as a child who has no alternative, and is learned concomitant with acquiring the local presuppositions and language of social knowing. The other culture is learned as an adult foreigner. The details of the new culture under study are focal and specified. The own-culture comparison base is left implicit. Had the features of the own-culture been made equally focal and explicit, had they been "studied" directly, the implicit comparison would often have been negated. But although this would be an improvement, the features of the own-culture would still seem more sensible, reasonable, intuitively comprehensible, and moral. Those of the foreign culture would tend to seem arbitrary, strange, puzzling, if not immoral. To correct this, in an earlier paper I made the following suggestion:

> *Triangulation through the own-culture bias of observers.* The achievement of useful "realistic" constructs in a science requires multiple methods focused on the diagnosis of the same construct from independent points of observation, through a kind of triangulation. This is required because the sense data or

meter readings are now understood as the result of a transaction in which both the observer (or meter) and the object of investigation contribute to the form of the data. With a single observation at hand, it is impossible to separate the subjective and the objective component. When, however, observations through separate instruments and separate vantage points can be matched as reflecting "the same" objects, then it is possible to separate out the components in the data due to observer (instrument) and observed. It turns out that this disentangling process requires both multiple observers (methods) and multiple, dissimilar, objects of study.

Applied to the study of the philosophy of a culture, this implies that our typical one-observer one-culture study is inherently ambiguous. For any given feature of the report it is equivocal whether or not it is a trait of the observer or a trait of the object observed. To correct this the ideal paradigm might be as shown in Figure 2(a).

In the most general model, two anthropologists from different cultures would each study a third and fourth culture. Of the four ethnographies resulting, the common attributes in ethnographies 1 and 3 not shared with 2 and 4 could be attributed to ethnographer A, the common attributes in 2 and 4 not elsewhere present to ethnographer B. Looking at row consistencies in the figure, the common attributes in ethnographies 1 and 2 not present in 3 and 4 could be attributed to culture C as "objectively" known. Attributes common to all four ethnographies are inherently ambiguous, interpretable as either shared biases on the part of the ethnographers or shared culture on the part of the societies studied. Note the desirability in this regard of comparing ethnologists with as widely differing cultural backgrounds as possible. Insofar as the ethnologists come from the same culture, the replication of

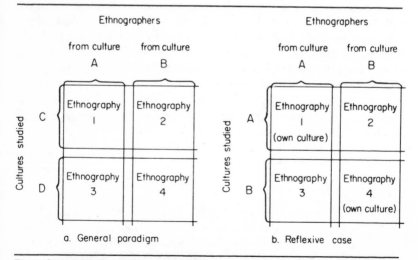

Figure 2: Multiple-Ethnography Schedules To Extricate the Ethnographer-Contributed Content from the Culture-Studied Content

results becomes more a matter of reliability than validity, as these terms are used in discussions of psychological tests. Were such a study carried out by using four ethnographers, two from each ethnographer cultures A and B, studying separate villages of cultures C and D to avoid interference and collusion, then the attributes unique to any one of the ethnographies would be attributable to an equivocal pool of village specificities within its culture, to personality specifics of the ethnographer, and interaction of specific ethnographer culture and studied culture. (If only one ethnologist were used from each culture, and if each of the two studied in turn the same village in the target cultures, then the features unique to any one of the four ethnographies would be equivocally due to ethnographer-culture interactions, time-order effects in which the ethnographer reacted differently to his second culture, time-order effects in which the society reacted differently to the second student of it, historical trends, and interactions among these.) The presence of these indeterminancies should neither be suppressed nor be allowed to overshadow the great gains in understanding which such multiple ethnographer studies would introduce.

While multiplicity of both ethnographer-cultures and cultures studied is ideal, it would also be a great gain to achieve only the upper half of Figure 2(a), i.e., two ethnographer-cultures focused on the study of a single target culture. In all such triangulations, we again face the paradox of inability to use differences when these so dominate as to make it impossible to match the corresponding aspects of the report being compared. The necessity of this common denominator provides one justification for Hockett's advocacy of including material and behavioral cultural details even in ethnographies focused on the determination of the philosophy of the cultures.

Another version of the multi-ethnographer, multiple-target design is that in which two cultures study each other, as diagramed in Figure 2(b). Usually the focus is on ethnographies 2 and 3, A's report on B and B's report on A. Implicitly, however, A's description of A and B's description of B are contained as bases of reference. There is probably some scientific value to be gained from such reports, even at the level of mutual stereotype sets or of reputational consensus from neighboring peoples. Once the evaluative component (each tribe viewing itself as best) is removed, such mutual stereotype sets show remarkable agreement in confirming the direction of group differences [Campbell, 1964: 331-333].

In line with the present discussion, I would now expand the requirements by asking that in a second phase of fieldwork, each ethnographer be asked to cross-validate, and invalidate, the other's interpretation of the culture they had studied in common.

CONCLUDING COMMENTS

This paper is obviously exploratory, an extreme oscillation away from my earlier dogmatic disparagement of case studies into another extreme equally one-sided. While it will not appreciably affect my own teaching about quasi-experimental designs and research methods, it does for the moment ring true. After all, man is, in his ordinary way, a very competent knower, and qualitative common-sense knowing is not replaced by quantitative knowing. Rather, quantitative knowing has to trust and build on the qualitative, including ordinary perception (Campbell, 1974). We methodologists must achieve an applied epistemology which integrates both.

REFERENCES

BACON, F. (1853) "Novum organum," in J. Devey (trans.) The Physical and Metaphysical Works of Lord Bacon. London: H. G. Bohn. (originally published in 1620)

BECKER, H. (1970) Sociological Work. Chicago: Aldine.

BOESCH, E. E. and L. H. ECKENSBERGER (1969) "Methodische Probleme des interkulterellen Vergleichs," pp. 515-566 in C. F. Graumann (ed.) Socialpsychologie. Gottingen: Verlag fur Psychologie.

BORING, E. G. (1954) "The nature and history of experimental control." American Journal of Psychology 67: 573-589.

CAMPBELL, D. T. (1974) "Qualitative knowing in action research." Kurt Lewin Award Address, Society for the Psychological Study of Social Issues, meeting with the American Psychological Association, New Orleans, September 1. (to appear, after revision, in Journal of Social Issues)

——— (1970) "Considering the case against experimental evaluations of social innovations." Administrative Science Quarterly 15: 110-113.

——— (1969) "A phenomenology of the other one: corrigible, hypothetical and critical," pp. 41-69 in T. Mischel (ed.) Human Action: Conceptual and Empirical Issues. New York: Academic Press.

——— (1966) "Pattern matching as an essential in distal knowing," pp. 81-106 in K. R. Hammond (ed.) The Psychology of Egon Brunswik. New York: Holt, Rinehart & Winston.

——— (1964) "Distinguishing differences of perception from failures of communication in cross-cultural studies," pp. 308-336 in F.S.C. Northrop and H. H. Livingston (eds.) Cross-Cultural Understanding: Epistemology in Anthropology. New York: Harper & Row.

——— (1961) "The mutual methodological relevance of anthropology and psychology," pp. 333-352 in F.L.K. Hsu (ed.) Psychological Anthropology: Approaches to Culture and Personality. Homewood, IL: Dorsey.

——— (1959) "Systematic error on the part of human links in communications systems." Information and Control 1: 334-369.

——— and J. C. STANLEY (1966) Experimental and Quasi-Experimental Designs for Research. Chicago: Rand McNally.

DuBOIS, C. A. (1944) The People of Alor. Minneapolis: University of Minnesota Press.

ERIKSON, E. H. (1950) Childhood and Society. New York: W. W. Norton.

——— (1943) Observations on the Yurok. Publications in American Archaeology and Ethnology, 35, No. 10. Berkeley: University of California Press.

——— (1939) "Observations on Sioux education." Journal of Psychology 7: 101-156.

GUTTENTAG, M. (1973) "Subjectivity and its use in evaluation research." Evaluation 1:

60-65.

—— (1971) "Models and methods in evaluation research." Journal for the Theory of Social Behavior 1: 75-95.

HELSON, H. (1964) Adaptation-Level Theory. New York: Harper & Row.

HSU, F.L.K. [ed.] (1961) Psychological Anthropology: Approaches to Culture and Personality. Homewood, IL: Dorsey.

KARDINER, A. (1939) The Individual and His Society. New York: Columbia University Press.

KENYATTA, J. (1938) Facing Mount Kenya. London: Secker & Warburg.

KIDDER, L. H. (1971) "Foreign visitors: a study of the changes in selves, skills, and attitudes of Westerners in India." Ph.D. dissertation, Northwestern University.

KROEBER, A. L. (1939) "Totem and taboo in retrospect." American Journal of Sociology 45: 446-451.

—— (1920) "Totem and taboo: an ethnological psychoanalysis." American Anthropologist 22: 48-55.

KROEBER, T. (1970) Alfred Kroeber: A Personal Configuration. Berkeley: University of California Press.

LASSWELL, H. D. (1968) "The future of the comparitive method." Comparative Politics 1: 3-18.

LIJPHART, A. (1971) "Comparative politics and the comparative method." American Political Science Review 65: 682-693.

LORD, F. M. and M. R. NOVICK (1968) Statistical Theories of Mental Test Scores. Reading, MA: Addison-Wesley.

MEEHL, P. E. (1967) "Theory-testing in psychology and physics: a methodological paradox." Philosophy of Science 34: 103-115.

NAROLL, R. (1962) Data Quality Control: A New Research Technique. New York: Free Press.

POINCARE, H. (1913) "Mathematical creation," in H. Poincare, The Foundations of Science. New York: Science Press.

RASER, J. R. (1969) Simulation and Society. Boston: Allyn & Bacon.

——, D. T. CAMPBELL, and R. W. CHADWICK (1970) "Gaming and simulation for developing theory relevant to international relations." General Systems 15: 183-204.

RYAN, T. A. (1960) "Significance tests for multiple comparisons of proportions, variances and other statistics." Psychological Bulletin 57: 318-328.

SALASIN, S. (1973) "Experimentation revisited: A conversation with Donald T. Campbell." Evaluation 1: 7-13.

SCHEFFE, H. (1953) "A method for judging all contrasts in analysis of variance." Biometrika 40: 87-104.

SEGALL, M. H., D. T. CAMPBELL, and M. J. HERSKOVITS (1966) The Influence of Culture on Visual Perception. Indianapolis: Bobbs-Merrill.

SELVIN, H. C. and A. STUART (1966) "Data-dredging procedures in survey analysis." American Statistician 20: 20-23.

STOUFFER, S. A. [ed.] (1949) The American Soldier: Princeton: Princeton University Press.

TOLMAN, E. C. and I. KRECHEVSKY (1933) "Means-end-readiness and hypothesis." Psychological Review 40: 60-70.

WEISS, R. S. and M. REIN (1970) "The evaluation of broad-aim programs: experimental design, its difficulties and an alternative." Administrative Science Quarterly 15: 97-109.

—— (1969) "The evaluation of broad-aim programs: a cautionary case and a moral." Annals of the American Academy of Political and Social Science 385: 133-142.

WYATT, D. F. and D. T. CAMPBELL (1951) "On the liability of stereotype or hypothesis." Journal of Abnormal and Social Psychology 46: 496-500.

4

M. G. Trend

Abt Associates Inc.

ON THE RECONCILIATION OF QUALITATIVE AND QUANTITATIVE ANALYSES
A Case Study

INTRODUCTION

This paper examines an instance where the analysis of qualitative data from a participant observer produced an explanation that could not be reconciled immediately with one based upon quantitative data drawn from the same social experiment. The presentation is undertaken with three purposes in mind.

First, the details of the case may give the reader some insight into the social psychology which operates in large-scale research efforts where the analytic work is performed by teams of workers from many different disciplines.

Second, the case may help to dispel the notion that using multiple methods will lead to sounder explanations in an easy, additive fashion. Indeed, the neat dovetailing of the pieces of a research puzzle should be cause for suspicion. Unanimity may be the hallmark of work in which the avenues to other explanations have been closed off prematurely.

Third, the confrontation between two different explanations of the same events and the eventual resolution of this conflict suggest a way of proceeding with other research that uses a multimethod perspective.

I feel that the proliferation of divergent explanations should be encouraged. Different analyses, each based upon a different form of information, should be kept separate until late in the analytic game.

Reproduced by permission of the Society for Applied Anthropology from *Human Organization,* 37: 345-354, 1978.

Alternative explanations should be allowed to "mature," and gain adherents or defenders. Then, the stories should be compared. If the accounts mesh, this provides an independent test of the validity of the research. If they do not, the areas of disagreement will provide points at which further analytic leverage can be exerted. A synthesis should be attempted. The desired result is a third explanation that is deductively derived, testable, and can account for all of the facts at hand.

THE CONTEXT

During 1972, the U.S. Department of Housing and Urban Development (HUD) undertook three social experiments designed to test the concept of using direct cash housing allowance payments to help low-income families obtain decent housing on the open market. By giving money to those in need, with the stipulation that the subsidy be spent on shelter, HUD hoped to use the existing housing stock more efficiently. In the process, assistance recipients could exercise freedom of choice by selecting their own units according to personal preference.

Two of the experiments were econometric. One was designed to measure the effects that a full-scale allowance program would have upon the local housing market in an urban area. The other focused upon how the recipients used their subsidies.

The third study, known as the Administrative Agency Experiment (AAE), sought to identify management issues associated with the direct cash assistance approach. Eight public agencies, located in different parts of the country, were to design and implement their own versions of a housing allowance program. Depending upon the size of the eligible population, each local project was authorized to serve as many as 900 families for up to two years. HUD selected Abt Associates Inc., a Cambridge-based research firm, to perform and evaluate the experiment. Its job was to determine which approaches worked best according to both the costs and effects of the different strategies and the experiences of agency staffs and program participants.

RESEARCH DESIGN

The AAE was a naturalistic experiment; it used no control or treatment groups. However, project planning, reporting, and data collection were organized around a set of twelve "functions." These were analytic constructs. Each one of them described an activity that an agency had to perform. Variation was encouraged, although within limits.

The analytic functions, made real by program practices, defined what was expected from all who were involved. Some of the functions, such as "Audit and Control," referred to purely administrative responsibilities. Others, such as "Inspection," could involve the participants directly. For example, although HUD had required that inspections be performed on all program units, local planners would decide who would perform these inspections. Hence, the variation in this one function alone ranged from using local code enforcement officials, to using agency housing counselors, to letting the participants themselves determine whether the housing they selected met minimum standards.

Proposed program designs were submitted to HUD, criticized, and revised. Negotiations culminated with the signing of funding contracts. After this had been done, the *contracting agencies*—as they came to be called—were required to create separate *administrative agencies* to implement the program. Abt Associates would observe, monitor, and evaluate the latter entities.

The information collected for the evaluation included both quantitative and qualitative data. A common set of six forms was used to track the progress of participating families. Employees charged their time to the appropriate functions on a daily basis. Agency accountants kept track of expenditures in much the same way. This and other information was sent to Abt Associates, where it was keypunched and loaded onto computer disks.

Teams of survey researchers interviewed a sample of participants and terminees at scheduled intervals. Both before and after their entry into the program, these participants had their current housing evaluated by Abt Associates, to see if those receiving benefits had actually moved to better units. Eventually, the quantitative data base would comprise more than 55 million *characters*.

An observer was assigned to each site for the first year of the experiment. The administrative agencies provided them with office space and allowed them to watch the program operations on a daily basis. Most of the observers were anthropologists. Their job was to provide the qualitative data for the study. Field notes and logs were completed and mailed to Cambridge at regular intervals; these eventually totaled more than 25,000 pages.

Three types of reports were envisioned by HUD and Abt Associates. The first consisted of comparative, cross-site function reports. They were to be based mostly on quantitative analysis and would evaluate program *outcomes*. Eight site case studies were planned as a second kind of product. These were designed as narrative, qualititively-based pieces that would enrich the function reports by providing a holistic picture of program *process* at the administrative agencies. A final report would then digest the findings of all the analyses and convert these into policy recommendations for a national housing allowance program.

THE CASE

Each AAAE site and its planned program were unique in some way. Site B was interesting for many reasons. First, the contracting agency was located 70 miles from the core of the program area. This suggested that the administrative agency might have to operate fairly independently.

Second, the program jurisdiction consisted of three non-contiguous areas. Two were rural counties; one was a medium-size city. To better serve the intended participants, three site offices were set up, and the urban one was designated as the headquarters. The existence of the branch offices raised the possibility of coordination problems.

Third, the contracting agency had never before been responsible for a grass-roots program. Some of the Cambridge-based researchers wondered if the transition would prove difficult, although the contracting agency appeared aggressive and anxious to succeed.

Fourth, the philosophy of the written plan reflected a mixture of participant independence and agency control. Few supportive services were to be offered. After a brief explanation about how to look for housing, each enrolled family was to be responsible for finding the kind of unit it wanted. Then—at least in the city—an agency inspection would be performed, using a stringent checklist. The written plan anticipated that fully 20% of the units would not pass muster.

The Site B program was designed with efficiency in mind. Performance goals were set, and the contracting agency required the central site office to monitor program progress carefully. They did not want things to stray off course. A particular concern was financial management. The contracting agency wanted theirs to be the *best* demonstration project in the AAE. In the words of a HUD official, the planners intended to run a "lean and mean" program.

FIELD OBSERVATIONS AND EXPLANATIONS

In the site observer's viewpoint, the smooth-running social program envisioned by the planners never materialized. Delays in signing the HUD contract caused the local offices to open a month behind schedule. Nevertheless, the site was required to adhere to the original timetable. Applications could be taken only for the first eight—now seven—months of the program. Site B would have to play catch-up, if they were to meet the program milestones and participation goals.

Initial response to the program had been slow. Since the contracting agency's central concern was serving the full 900 families, it ordered increased outreach efforts to get more people to apply. However, three or four months passed before families came to the program in numbers.

Early monitoring by the contracting agency had shown that the effort was farthest behind in the urban portion of the program area. They gauged "progress" primarily by the number of households receiving payments at any one time. The regulations allowed a household to receive benefits only if it met certain requirements within 90 days after enrollment. Within this period, a household had to locate an acceptable unit—it could be the one in which it was already living—and arrange for an inspection. Only if the housing met the minimum standards and the landlord agreed to sign a year's lease could payments be initiated.

In the rural area, most enrollees seemed to be meeting the program requirements easily. In contrast, those in the city were dropping out in high proportions without ever qualifying for a subsidy. The experimental program was falling even farther behind schedule and the contracting agency decided to look for a new solution.

The solution they chose was to increase the number of enrollees as quickly as possible to make up for the attrition. They imposed daily processing quotas on each worker. In order to meet them, the counselors began to enroll selected applicants in groups rather than individually.

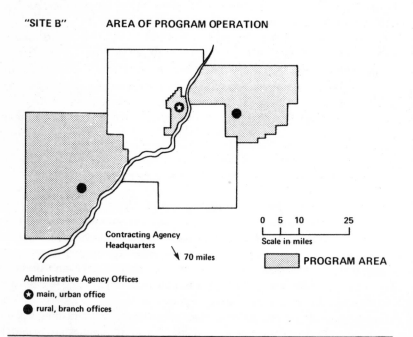

"SITE B"   AREA OF PROGRAM OPERATION

Contracting Agency
Headquarters
↘ 70 miles

0   5   10   25
Scale in miles

PROGRAM AREA

Administrative Agency Offices
✪ main, urban office
● rural, branch offices

Figure 1: Site B. Area of Program Operation

Contracting agency managers visited the administrative agency frequently to make sure that their wishes for increased activity were being carried out.

The housing counselors complained that they had become mere paper-pushers, and that group enrollments did not allow them to establish working relationships with their clients. Nevertheless, the counselors also eliminated any hint of counseling or supportive services. Previously, enrollees were required to attend a meeting where they could discuss how to find good housing. Now, they were advised only of the technical requirements they had to meet if they were to receive a subsidy.

The administrative agency staff began to complain of overwork. The housing counselor in charge of inspections in the urban area felt that he was being pressured to pass marginal units just so the program could meet its goal of 900 recipients. The plan called for 650 of them to come from within the city limits, where the worst housing was located. Further, as the masses of enrollees began to find housing, inspections to be done came in bunches. The housing counselor in charge of inspections felt this could have been avoided if people had been admitted into the program at a controlled rate.

The main office staff was sure that recipients had found "junk housing." After all, most poor people had been living in dilapidated units all of their lives. They would not even know what to look for when they chose a new apartment.

Personality conflicts arose within the administrative agency staff at the main office. They felt that they had to compete with each other in order to meet their quotas and save their jobs. Some of the counselors privately admitted that they had become sloppy in their verification of enrollee incomes. Many of them worried that cases of participant fraud would later be uncovered.

Much hostility was directed outward, toward the contracting agency staff who had imposed the processing quotas, and toward the program director who enforced these measures. The housing counselors complained that the approach they were taking was inhumane, and noted that many needy enrollees were failing to receive benefits because they simply could not find housing. One of the program planners retorted, "You don't wear your heart on your sleeve in this program."

The atmosphere in the rural offices was quite different. Although the people there worked hard, no one complained of too much to do. The rural staff had even found time to make home visits and inspect all recipient units. This had not been called for in the plan. They just wanted to make sure things were all right. And they were. Main office staff and the observer envied the warm relations among workers at the satellite offices. These were attributed generally to a lack of contracting agency interference and to the geographical and emotional distance of the rural staff from the conflict at the main site office. If any complaint came from the staff in outlying regions of the program, it was that they felt isolated.

The field notes and logs from the Site B observer recorded the conflict that was occurring between the contracting agency and the main site office. These were read avidly by the in-house analysts of Abt Associates. Whenever the eight observers were called back to Cambridge for briefings, Site B was discussed at length.

The Cambridge analysis staff was split on the relevance of the conflict. Some argued that it was idiosyncratic to the site, and hence, of little policy importance. Others felt that there might be structural causes to the friction. Difficulties in long-distance management were suggested as a possibility. The observer felt that the lack of harmony was a case of managerial incompetence compounded by strong personalities within both agencies.

Only one of the senior analysts was suspicious of the observer's accounts. He felt that operations at Site B appeared "chaotic," and this confused him. He noted that the program looked as if it might serve the full 900 households, however badly, and that even this must take some ability and coordination.

Delays in coding and cleaning the hard data prevented any further light from being shed on recipient housing quality, demography of program dropouts, or cost of running such a program. The observer was sent back to the site with instructions to find out more about the discord. Towards the end of the enrollment period, he did. He reported that the personality conflicts at the site had now taken on racial overtones.

As in most public assistance programs, minorities had oversubscribed to the housing allowance project at Site B. The contracting agency wanted to have a demographically balanced project which served different types of households according to their representation in the eligible population. HUD had required that each agency estimate the minority population in the program area, to be sure that minorities were not underrepresented in the experiment. The contracting agency felt that meeting these population profiles would serve as a measure of the effectiveness of their efforts. Therefore, the order was given to curtail enrollment of Black households, as they were already too heavily represented among the enrollees.

Black staff members and a number of liberal White housing counselors were outraged. They felt that the program should operate on a first-come basis. Further, they wanted to give more services to enrollees—particularly Blacks—who they knew were having a hard time finding housing. The angry staff members argued that even if only 500 families were to receive benefits, the extra counseling and personalized attention would assure that everyone enrolled in the program got decent housing. In this way, the program could still be termed a "success," even if full participation had not been achieved.

The contracting agency held fast and insisted on the primacy of numerical and demographic goals. They implored the urban office to continue enrolling more White families—and to do it faster.

Eventually, 900 households did receive payments. However, the disillusioned housing counselors felt both that the program was de facto racist, and that they had been pushed beyond their limits by an assembly line approach toward a housing allowance program. Many of these employees resigned after the end of the enrollment period, well ahead of the termination dates on their contracts.

WRITING IT DOWN

The above account gives the viewpoint of both the Site B observer and many of the staff at the urban site office. It formed the basis of a 35-page "essence paper." Written as a prelude to the actual case study, its purpose was to provide an overview of the site; to capture the "essence" of the local administrative agency. As manager of the case studies—and a former observer at another site—I had requested that each observer write such a paper in order to clarify his thoughts. These were completed six months after the observers had left the sites.

Reviewers of the Site B essence paper were only somewhat disappointed that the piece had used personality conflicts and managerial incompetence to explain what had gone on at the site. While it made for engaging reading, the account merely chronicled staff dissensions and predicted that, if judged by any other criteria than that of servicing 900 households, the Site B program was a failure. Early analysis of recipient housing quality improvement seemed to bear out this contention.

The observer was told to start his case study, and to try to cover agency procedures more completely. The emphasis upon office strife had obscured how the program actually worked function by function. The Cambridge analysts felt that information on the performance of the functions would best contribute to the design of a national housing program. If the staff conflict was largely personal or idiosyncratic, this was of no relevance to policy makers. The observer was also instructed to rewrite the essence paper, since it would serve as an informal report to HUD on research in progress. Finally, although Cambridge staff admitted that contracting agency personnel had been close-mouthed and inaccessible, they suggested strongly that the observer try to understand their performance-oriented viewpoint, and give it some consideration.

CONFLICTING EXPLANATIONS

It took an additional five months for the Site B case study and essence paper to be completed. They were presented, reviewed, and rejected. This time the problem was more serious. The quantitative data base had been cleaned and "frozen." Based upon new computer runs, the *outcome measures* seemed to show that Site B had performed quite well compared with the other sites. The cost model indicated that the Site B program had been cheap to run. Revised calculations of site demography showed that minorities were appropriately represented in the recipient population. Moreover, for all of the reports of staff dissension, no effect upon the recipients could be discerned. The image of the Site B program that was forming in the minds of the in-house analysts was one of a well-managed social program that had met its own and other performance measures. Only the improvement in housing quality remained in doubt. "What if this turns out to be our best site?" someone asked.

The new essence paper no longer focused upon personal disagreements. Instead, it now depicted staff overwork and the heavy-handed interference of a contracting agency that wanted to succeed at any price. However, based upon the results of the quantitative analysis, the actions of the contracting agency managers—even if they were self-serving—could not be dismissed as incompetent or inappropriate. They had achieved results. At worst, the managers could be faulted for their abrasiveness and insensitivity, but neither was a crime.

The problem with the essence paper was now twofold. First, the piece still contained references to discord, none of which—in the absence of any program effect—was policy relevant. Second, the quantitative analysis was telling a different story from the one in the essence paper. Since the quantitative data were gathered under prescribed conditions, and were subjected to uniform "stimuli" or operations, the analysis based upon them was thought to be reliable. The Cambridge analysts felt that the qualitative data could not easily be checked for reliability. The ways in which field-workers drew their inferences were not explicit, and their decision rules were individualistic and hidden. Now, in the face of conflicting explanations, the credibility of the Site B observer began to be questioned.

An increasing number of Cambridge staff believed that the observer "had an ax to grind." He was suspected of having been caught up in office politics and of having lost his scientific objectivity. His mildly reformist outlook made him even more suspect, and senior staff regretted the freedom they had given him. The analysts were sure that the qualitative equivalent of "measurement bias" had occurred. The observer was an "instrument" that was measuring the wrong thing—staff conflict. I had access to the field notes and disagreed. I felt "measurement error" was the problem; the observer had not probed deeply enough.[1] Therefore, I agreed to help with the rewriting of the essence paper.

The observer and I did what most researchers would do when faced with mounting evidence that their dearly held interpretations were wrong: we capitulated and tried to salvage whatever scraps of the original explanation we could. Three more drafts were produced. The first skirted the issue of conflict, and tried to concentrate on a description of local context and the way the functions were performed at Site B. This version was rejected with a scrawled note: "What do we want to do? Get a report out, or take a trip?" Another try yielded a paper that talked about the "by-the-numbers" mindset of the program planners. However, the threads of the story were lost as we were confronted by more and more hard analysis that showed no ill effects from this. The hard analysis was leading the soft. We gave it chase, trying to keep up with the new findings.

The fifth and final versions portrayed how the contracting agency had legitimately emphasized the income maintenance aspects of the direct cash assistance approach at the expense of improved housing quality for recipients. The lack of harmony at Site B was explained away as being the result of two different opinions on what the program should accomplish. The view held by the contracting agency was concerned with programmatic ends, or outcomes. The other, held by the administrative agency staff, was more humane, and was concerned with the living conditions of participants. *Unfortunately, just as we had finished this version of the essence paper, new quantitative analysis showed that Site B recipients enjoyed an improvement in housing quality that ranked second in the AAE.*

Sides began to be chosen. The Site B observer insisted that his interpretation was basically correct. He knew what he had seen. The other former observers had heard rumors about the trouble with the Site B essence paper, and defended their colleague. One of them felt that the problem was a political one, and opined that the original essence paper "told it like it was, but Abt Associates is afraid to print it." Another asserted that outcome measures did not tell the whole truth, that quantitative techniques were "garbage" and that human behavior could not be reduced to "mere numbers."[2]

The observer was by now thoroughly discredited in the eyes of the Cambridge staff. Even though he had softened his views about the contracting agency, he was still thought to be both biased and stubborn. The observer was relieved of his responsibilities. Although he would still assist me, I was to be in charge of producing another essence paper from scratch.

I felt partially responsible for the observer's downfall, and said so. The other Cambridge analysts assured me that I would feel better "once things were turned around."

THE SYNTHESIS[3]

The curious thing, I thought, was that neither side seriously doubted "the facts" uncovered by either method of inquiry. The problem seemed to be one of different interpretations of those facts, only some of which were shared. To be sure, quantitative analysts placed more stock in the hard outcome measures. On the other hand, the observer had his 18 months on site to draw upon. The same social field, viewed from different perspectives, seemed to produce explanations that might as well have been based on two different realities. It seemed reminiscent of the Japanese movie, "Rashomon." The observer and I called the puzzlement the "Rashomon effect."

We had to answer the question of how a program could produce such admirable results in so many of its aspects, when all of the observational data indicated that the program would be a failure. What had happened, and how?

Although both data bases—hard and soft—were now complete, I did not know where to start. A confrontation with the senior analyst who had been the most vocal in his criticisms produced an insight. After the rejection of the last essence paper, I asked him what—besides the housing quality measures—had made him doubt the observer's interpretations. He said that he was suspicious of the protestations of overwork that he had read about: "They don't put in any overtime; they don't ask for extra help. All they do is complain." Then he added, "I think 'overwork' is a smoke-screen. They sound like they're alienated."

I offered that we could test whether the workloads at Site B were inordinately high. The hard data base would allow us to track the flow of participants into the program on a monthly basis. We could then calculate how much processing the operations staff had to do. The same could be done for all of the sites, and comparisons could be made.

I mentioned several other areas where the qualitative and quantitative explanations diverged. I was particularly suspicious of the contention that the monitoring at Site B was a model of precision. The observer's field notes had described the casual manner in which eligible applicants had been selected for enrollment, and the agency's obsession with recipient milestones that bordered on the mystical. Yet, the outcome measures seemed to suggest that site monitoring had been neat, precise, and rational. I wondered if it wasn't possible for a program to stumble into "success," and I wanted to test this idea.

The observer and I worked together on the reanalysis for six weeks. The results took another month to write up. Half jokingly, we made four pompously-stated rules that would guide our inquiry:

(1) No fact will be ignored for the sake of a cleaner explanation.
(2) All hypotheses must be cast in a refutable form.
(3) We will specify beforehand, as much as possible, the conditions under which we will abandon a belief.
(4) Falsified hypotheses have to be replaced by other, alternative explanations, which will themselves be tested.

Testing staff workloads proved to be time consuming, but not taxing. With the help of a computer, we were able to recreate on paper the flow of applicants, enrollees, and recipients at all of the sites. The levels at Site B were somewhat higher, although only for a month or two. Yet the mass-production approach of Site B suggested that each case processed there probably took much less time than at any other agency in the AAE. Furthermore, the complaints about "overwork" had begun quite early in the main office, long before the worst of the enrollee build-up.

Since the character of the rural offices had seemed so different to the observer, we split Site B into its three components. Things began to look more interesting. We found that on a per-person basis, one of the rural site offices had processed almost as many households as the main office. Yet the rural site people had not complained of having to work too hard, and had even expanded their duties by giving more and more attention to each family in their part of the program.

"Alienation" began to look more attractive as an explanation of the discontent in the main office. Most of the operations workers had social service backgrounds; they wanted to help people in need. With little explanation, the contacting agency had ordered them to push more and more people into the program. Housing counselors were discouraged from providing services, the job that they thought they had been hired to do. No such constraints had been placed on the workers in the rural areas. There, program milestones were being met and the contracting agency saw no need to interfere.

We examined staff alienation further. Because receiving full funding from HUD was contingent upon having 900 households receiving payments, the staff's insistence that the program would run just as well if it served only 500 families indicated a lack of understanding of the fiscal aspects of the experiment. The field notes and logs supported this assertion, and the observer was positive that the need for a balanced budget, and how this could be achieved, had never been explained by the contracting agency. In fact, he hadn't quite understood it all himself. Thus, at the main office— where the effort was running behind schedule—the housing counselors were being required to enroll in huge numbers in order to get 900 recipients by the end of the enrollment period, without knowing *why* full participation was so important.

Site monitoring procedures were examined. We knew that it was possible for a local program to run out of money if the amount of the average housing allowance rose above planned levels because each recipient household, according to its size alone, generated a certain amount of money that was paid to the agency. Money for staff salaries and office expenses came from this "pot." However, each housing allowance was figured according to a mathematical formula whose terms included both household size and family income.[4] Therefore, even if an agency had achieved full participation, it could still come up short. The easiest way for an agency to go bankrupt was to have it serve *only* very low income households. If this happened, all of the money would be paid out in subsidies and none would be left over for administrative expenditures.

In the urban area, where most of the recipients lived, the agency had not been able to keep housing allowance levels within permissible limits. This was in part because many of the recipients were minority group members whose household size and income entitled them to high payments. The decision to cut back on Black enrollments, coupled with a high percentage of Blacks who dropped out in the enrollee stage because they could not find housing, kept finances from getting even further out of hand at the main office. However, the decision to curtail the enrollment of minorities was made for the *wrong* reason—to have a "racially balanced" program.

In contrast, enrollees in the rural areas were White. As many as 80% of them reached recipient status, compared with 51% of the urban blacks. The White households were smaller in size, had higher incomes, and thus qualified for lower than average payments. Inclusion of these families had the effect of reducing the average subsidy paid and—in effect—made more funds available for administrative purposes. By treating Site B as a single piece the quantitative analysts had missed almost all of what we now were discovering.[5]

We also found that the files at the main office had not been carefully kept. Only once during the enrollment period were households that had exceeded the 90-day housing search period terminated from the program. This meant that neither the contracting agency nor the administrative agency could have known how many people were looking for housing at any one time or how they were faring. When the payments milestones were not being met on schedule, the contracting agency ordered the main office to enroll more households more quickly. The actual selections were made by "eyeballing" a list of applicants, and the income and household size information which guided this process had not been verified and was often inaccurate.

We were now certain that the apparent efficiency of the Site B operations was, in part, illusory. There was no gain-saying the exemplary outcomes of the local effort. However, the housing market had worked in the agency's favor, at least as far as the budget was concerned. In a different setting, the same techniques of program monitoring and control might have proved disastrous. As it was, the dropout rate among Black enrollees in the urban area was the second highest in the AAE.

Ironically, the alienation of the staff at the main office, which had been engendered by poor communications from the contracting agency, helped lower costs further. Since the disgruntled employees had left ahead of schedule, money budgeted for salaries could be used to defray other expenses.

After we had examined further the enrollment strategy of the contracting agency, we realized that the low "unit costs" were telling a slanted story to the in-house analysts. Some of the efficiency measures were based upon the cost per enrollee. The contracting agency had deliberately enrolled as many households as it could. The crudest of the measures ignored, and could not quantify, the wastage that occurred when a household was enrolled but dropped out because it could not find housing within the 90-day time limit.[6] Further, the mass-production methods employed by the agency meant that a larger number of households could be handled by a relatively small staff, adding to the illusion of "efficiency." We now felt that the Cambridge analysts had approached the evaluation with their own built-in biases.

At some point in our new analytic effort, a "lift-off stage" was reached. The observer and I no longer felt hampered by either of the earlier, conflicting interpretations of what happened at Site B. Although we still occasionally referred to previous work, our tested hypotheses seemed to suggest other areas for investigation. We felt only mildly constrained by the dictum that everything we had to say should be of immediate and obvious policy relevance.

We were puzzled by the fact that the proportion of enrollees that reached recipient status varied among all of the three subareas of the program jurisdiction, even after we had controlled for race. The success rate for White enrollees was not the same for the three site offices.

Figures from the 1970 Census indicated that the rental vacancy rate was almost uniformly low across the entire program area. Therefore, we ruled out market conditions as an explanation of why the success rate for White households differed. Only after we looked at the moving intentions of the enrollees did we find an answer. The rural county which had the largest percentage of households wanting to stay in their original units also had the largest proportion of enrollees who qualified for payments. The city had the lowest proportion on both accounts. The other rural county fell in between.

The finding was extraneous to the arguments in the essence paper and was never written up. However, later analysis confirmed that people who intended to move, and presumably looked for housing, were in an "at-risk" category at all AAE sites with tight housing markets. Analytic work for another report later showed that supportive services helped White enrollees in such markets attain recipient status. Further, high levels of services helped minority households to qualify for housing regardless of their moving intention or local market conditions (cf. Wild 1977). In retrospect, this lent credence to the Site B housing counselors' contention that giving more personal assistance to enrollees may have made for lower attrition rates and a more humane program.

After our work was largely completed, we found that we did not have enough information to adequately test certain areas of disagreement between the qualitative and quantitive analyses. A small residue of unexplained findings would remain. The high housing quality attained by Site B recipients was something we could not refute with the qualitative data. However, we were still suspicious of this outcome, and we hedged on it. We wrote that, whatever kinds of units Site B recipients were living in, they had found the housing themselves, with little help or interference from the administrative agency. This proved to be a prudent conclusion: later—much later—the housing quality measure employed by in-house analysts was shown to be faulty.[7]

The acceptable version of the essence paper involved no real heroes or villains. To be sure, the contracting agency had employed draconian measures to make certain that performance goals were met. Some of the objectives were appropriate, others were questionable, and still others were just plain wrong or silly. For all their emphasis on precision, the contracting agency managers had monitored the program poorly, and at no time were they really in control of the outcomes.

On the other hand, the administrative agency staff was unimaginative and had given up very early in the program. When faced with the need to make payments to 900 households, they were able to think of no other reasonable way of proceeding. Instead, they piously talked about giving extensive services to 500 families and serving these few people well—thus turning away an additional 400 needy households.

For their part, the recipient families seemed to like the program. If nothing else, the extra money helped their rent burden, regardless of the physical condition of the houses they were occupying. Major gains from the Site B efforts accrued to the in-house analysts of Abt Associates. They began to think of ways that conflicting interpretations could be used for gains in understanding.

CONCLUSIONS

The Administrative Agency Experiment involved at least five sets of actors or entities: the agencies, the program participants, the observers, the in-house analysts of Abt Associates, and HUD. Each represents a different level from which the experiment may be viewed.[8] For purposes of simplicity, I have focused upon one site, one observer, and the Cambridge analysts. I have also left out numbers and equations, as well as the contextual richness of the observational data. However, some points warrant stressing.

It may be tempting to say that the "Rashomon effect" experienced with the Site B analyses was caused by conflicting, disparate *data bases*. It was not. The difficulty lay in conflicting explanations or accounts, each based largely upon a different *kind* of data. The problems we faced involved not only the nature of observational *versus* statistical inferences, but two sets of preferences and biases within the entire research team. The solution was to overturn the existing explanations by offering a third. This required no brilliance, some ingenuity, and a good amount of tenacity.

Though qualitative/quantitative tension is not the only problem which may arise in research, I suggest that it is a likely one. Few researchers are equally comfortable with both types of data, and the procedures for using the two together are not well developed. The tendency is to relegate one type of analysis or the other to a secondary role, according to the nature of the research and the predilections of the investigators. I leave to methodologists the question of which type of information is useful for what kinds of problems.[9] Commonly, however, observational data are used for "generating hypotheses," or "describing *process*." Quantitative data are used to "analyze *outcomes*," or "verify hypotheses." I feel that this division of labor is rigid and limiting.

Conflict within a research team is painful. Since the desired end of analytic work is to produce a unified account or at least one consisting of smoothly fitted pieces, confrontations are almost deliberately avoided. The easiest way to do this honestly is never to give differing viewpoints a chance to arise.

"Grounded theory" (cf. Glaser and Strauss 1967), when carried to its logical extremes, stifles analytic dialogue in the interest of "science." Adherents to this doctrine believe that theory and explanation can best be formulated inductively, rather than deductively. The method involves constant reference to the events occurring in the social field under scrutiny. Bits and pieces of the explanatory framework are modified until they finally become congruent with "the facts."

An attendant danger of the grounded theory approach is that the explanations which emerge will be so ad hoc and so ingrown that they may negate any gains that can be realized by employing multiple methods and perspectives. Inductively derived explanations are more likely to be patchwork and jerry-built than they are elegant or refutable. Their generalizable quality is also lost.

Even if one does not take the headlong flight into grounded theory, one encounters additional pitfalls associated with multimethod research. It is now thoughtful to say that different methods of inquiry may be complementary (cf. Bennett and Thais 1970). The case presented here has shown that the complementarity is not always apparent. Simply using different perspectives, with the expectation that they will validate each other, does not tell what to do if the pieces do not fit.

This paper has endorsed the notion of *triangulation,* an idea put forth by Denzin (1970). Triangulation involves bringing a variety of data and methods to bear upon the same problem. In this way, sounder explanations can be produced. I suggest that we give different viewpoints the chance to arise, and postpone the immediate rejection of information or hypotheses that seem out of joint with the majority viewpoint.

Observationally derived explanations are particularly vulnerable to dismissal without a fair trial. This is because the data on which they are based are difficult to check for reliability. Had the discrepancies concerning the accounts of the Site B program been discovered while the observer was still in the field, he would have been nudged toward bringing his observations and conclusions into line with those of the rest of the research team. No coercion would have been involved. The observer would have been overwhelmed by the analysis that was based upon the eminently believable "hard" data.

It was a happy accident (but one which could be regularized) that the conflicting accounts of the Site B program were kept separate and allowed to gain strength. As it was, the observer and I "gave in" somewhat during the writing of the third, fourth, and fifth drafts of the essence paper. However, each side held so tightly to its own views that it was impossible to brush aside the lack of congruence, especially after the supposedly weaker viewpoint had been set down in a report. We were forced to dig more deeply to find out where the problem lay. Earlier harmony would have prevented any additional searching, since nothing would have needed explaining.

The resultant explanation accounted for almost all of the known facts, and had policy implications for the design of a housing allowance program. (If nothing else, the proper placement of monitoring points is something which can be written into regulations and explained in program operators' handbooks.) At the same time, I have no doubt that better interpretations of "what happened at Site B" can be fashioned, especially if new information comes to light.

The final version of the Site B essence paper was a modest achievement.[10] Nevertheless, the process by which it was produced approximated the conduct of science in one very important way. The puzzle-solving part of our effort was not its most important feature. This had gone on through all of the earlier analyses, both qualitative and quantitative. The juxtaposition of contradictory explanatory schemes provided the impetus for seeking a better, less inductive interpretation of Site B operations; one that was not bound by earlier preconceptions. The value of such confrontations had been noted by the philosopher of science, Paul Feyerabend:

It seems, then, that the interplay between tenacity and profileration (is) an essential feature in the actual development of science. It seems that it is not the puzzle-solving activity that is responsible for the growth of our knowledge, but the active interplay of various tenaciously held views. (1970: 209).

These sentiments are endorsed by another philosopher, one whose main contributions lie outside the field of philosophy of science. He recommended letting "a hundred flowers bloom and a hundred schools of thought contend . . ." (Mao 1967: 302).

To such pleas for methodological and interpretive hedonism, I add, "Yes, but test, test, test!"

NOTES

1. I am indebted to Dr. Robert Herriott, who told me the correct technical terms (i.e., "measurement error" and "measurement bias") to describe the two different views of what had happened with the observational data from Site B.

2. In the field of psychology, similar feelings are often expressed by clinicians who like to prescribe therapies on a patient-by-patient basis. A study done by Meehl (1954) found that statistical methods were superior to the clinicians' intuitions for predicting the efficacy and appropriateness of the assigned treatments.

3. The synthesis touched on points other than the ones presented here. For purposes of economy, I have confined myself to dealing with the most central areas of the conflicting interpretations.

4. The payments formula was:
$$HAP = C^* - .25 \, Y_{ag}$$
where
   HAP = the amount of the monthly housing allowance; and
   C^* = the estimated average gross rent of a modest unit for a family of a given size; and
   Y_{ag} = the total, monthly household income, less certain deductions.

5. I have no firm explanation of why Site B was treated as a whole for the quantitative analysis. One plausible reason is that most of the other sites had homogeneous program areas which usually consisted of a single city. The researchers may not have considered examining each subarea of Site B separately. Another plausible explanation is that, for much of the analytic work, only a sample of the participants at each site was used. By dividing the site into three parts, this may have reduced the N to below acceptable levels.

6. For a detailed examination of administrative costs in a housing allowance program, see Maloy et al. (1977).

7. The in-house analysts were unable to devise a satisfactory measure of housing quality. Instead, the report for this area of concern focused upon the adequacy of housing inspections (cf. Budding 1977).

8. I thank Prof. M. Penn, University College, University of Minnesota, for pointing this out to me.

9. Texts on methodology abound; for a good summary of the traditional uses of qualitative and quantitative data, cf. Whyte and Alberti (1976).

10. It is appropriate to note that the AAE was problem-oriented research. The "theoretical" schemes of the researchers were not as explicit as they might have been, had this been basic research. Nevertheless, even if different and implicit theoretical perspectives were the *sole* cause of the conflicting accounts, this still would not have relieved us of trying to make sense out of the two explanations.

REFERENCES

BENNETT, J. W. and G. THAIS (1970) "Survey research in anthropological field work," in R. Naroll and R. Cohen (eds.) A Handbook of Method in Cultural Anthropology. New York: Columbia University Press.

BUDDING, D. (1977) Inspection: Implementing Housing Quality Requirements in a Housing Allowance Program. Cambridge, MA: Abt.

DENZIN, N. K. (1970) The Research Act. Chicago: Aldine.

FEYERABEND, P. (1970) "Consolations for the specialist," in I. Lakatos and A. E. Musgrave (eds.) Criticism and the Growth of Knowledge. Cambridge: Cambridge University Press.

GLASER, B. G. and A. L. STRAUSS (1967) The Discovery of Grounded Theory: Strategies for Qualitative Research. Chicago: Aldine.

MALOY, C. M., J. P. MADDEN, D. BUDDING, and W. L. HAMILTON (1977) Administrative Costs in a Housing Program: Two Year Costs in the Administrative Agency Experiment. Cambridge, MA: Abt.

MAO TSE-TUNG (1967) Quotations from Chairman Mao Tse-Tung. Peking: Foreign Language Press.

MEEHL, P. E. (1954) Clinical Versus Statistical Prediction. Minneapolis: University of Minnesota Press.

WHYTE, W. F. and G. ALBERTI (1976) Power, Politics, and Progress. New York: Elsevier.

WILD, B. (1977) "The effects of agency services on enrollees' success in becoming recipients," in W. L. Holshouser (ed.) Supportive Services in a Housing Allowance Program. Cambridge: MA: Abt.

Francis A.J. Ianni
Margaret Terry Orr
Horace Mann-Lincoln Institute
Teachers College Columbia University

5

TOWARD A RAPPROCHEMENT OF QUANTITATIVE AND QUALITATIVE METHODOLOGIES

Over the last decade, there has been a steadily increasing interest among educators in qualitative measurement and in the use of field methods in educational research. To a considerable extent this interest grows out of the Civil Rights Act of 1964, which pushed education, and consequently the research which informs it, into a concern with cultural as well as individual differences. To some extent it is the result of dissatisfaction among the clients of educational research who tend to see traditional educational research paradigms as abstractions from the reality of the everyday life of schools. To some extent it also results from the growing sophistication of educational researchers themselves as they begin to explore methodologies other than those which developed during education's long and incestuous relationship with psychology.

This new interest in qualitative methods is not without problems. The demands which are being placed on qualitative methods by educators are major ones; in many cases they include expectations of problem solution and educational utility which are beyond the capabilities of current field research methods in education. At the same time, the long tradition of dominance that educational psychologists have exercised over educational research has produced a climate alien to the style and pace of ethnographic field studies. Also, anthropologists, the principal exponents of ethnographic research have been involved in educational research for too short a time to have developed systematic theory and methods in educational anthropology itself.

AUTHORS' NOTE: *Parts of this chapter were originally prepared for a report on anthropology and educational research for the National Academy of Education.*

QUALITATIVE METHODS IN EVALUATION

Evaluation today has become a major activity of social service programs. Within education, evaluation plays a leading role in research and development activities. Governmental agencies, Congress, and the public are concerned with educational activity and its effectiveness. As demands for good evaluation increase, however, so does the impact of poor evaluation. New demands of both educational programs and evaluation sponsors have brought about the current widespread dissatisfaction with past methodology. The customary use of quantitative data, for example, may provide much useful information on student achievement. But there is growing evidence that quantitative data cannot supply satisfactory answers to many of the qualitative questions of education today. It is no longer enough to say that Johnny can't read; what is now being asked is why he can't and what will make him learn. With this increasing dissatisfaction over current evaluation methods, two new attemps to refocus the more traditional types of evaluation have emerged, both with important implications for qualitative assessment.

One has been a swing in the unit of analysis from a focus on the *individual* as learner to a focus on the *program* as teacher. Early evaluation designs placed the major—and sometimes exclusive—emphasis on psychometric testing of students. The design was as simplistic as it was rational: if the goal of the program was to familiarize students with a specific body of information, then the best way to determine the success or failure of the program was to test those students to see if they had indeed acquired that information. So long as evaluation played a minor role in education, largely restricted to research concerns, this method did not present problems. In the 1960s, however, educational consumerism became a prominent movement and older evaluation methods no longer sufficed. Billions of dollars poured into education programs for the culturally deprived. Ghetto parents alleged that standard tests were culturally biased. The effectiveness of the tests in measuring program success was challenged. A major confrontation came when the Westinghouse Learning Corporation gave poor marks to the Head Start program, because achievement tests indicated little significant student progress. The Head Start program, then popular both in Congress and in urban communities, remains popular today. Westinghouse's challenge to the program met with sharp public criticism of the company's evaluation standards, and threw current evaluation techniques into the arena of public debate. For the first time, evaluation methodology was seriously questioned by people outside the profession. Evaluators were forced to shift away from a focus on individuals to a focus on programs. In so doing, agencies began looking to anthropology and "soft" sociology for techniques with which to observe and assess programs.

The second attempt to refocus evaluation design also came about when social programs began to acquire great quantities of money. When the passing of Title I of the Elementary and Secondary Education Act of 1965 brought the sudden investment of billions of dollars in inner city education, Congress became concerned with how the money would be spent. It was the evaluation component in the Elementary and Secondary Education Act which led both to the rapid growth of evaluation and to the commonplace requirement of a system of financial monitoring in evaluation. Because so much of the new money in education and educational research was pumped into urban (primarily ghetto) areas, questions of the effects of culture, subculture, race, ethnicity, and other features of the community became extremely important. The established procedures of close experimental control, control groups, and the logico-deductive process in general began to falter as these new concerns emerged. Clearly the laboratory-oriented style of research, which was part of the tradition of educational research, was not satisfactory for the evaluation of either ethnic studies programs or effective programs of education. Again, anthropology, which had always been concerned with the issues underlying such programs, provided a potential source of methodology.

Not all of the pressures for change, however, came from education. There had been growing dissatisfaction with evaluation studies of all persuasions because the standard practice produced a summative assessment which said, in effect, "Here is what you have done; here is what was wrong with it; if you ever do it again here are some suggestions which you might want to follow." In the new endeavors, evaluators required formative evaluation components in addition to what was previously only summative evaluation. Rather than being above and beyond the program, the evaluator was compelled to become a part of the program.

Most educators and many educational researchers agree that modern evaluation technology is in a sorry state. It still tends to be placed under the rubric of research and thereby has forced upon it the canons of science which are in many cases not applicable. Most evaluations today are *not* research but rather ad hoc attempts to provide some basis for describing and assessing programs, and accounting for expenditures of funds. Methods of testing come from psychology, techniques for program monitoring are borrowed from systems analytic procedures, methods of qualitative observation are adopted from sociology and anthropology, and all are hurriedly thrown together to make a deadline. Despite the fact that evaluators persist in referring to evaluation as research, none of the requirements of sound research seem to operate there. There is no theory to inform methodology, there is no consistency in methodological development, there is no systematic application of methods, and, perhaps most important, there is no system by which what is learned in one evaluation informs the next evaluator.

The primary reason for the discrepancy between evaluation means and ends stems from education's failure to develop a consistent evaluation methodology which uniquely fits education. The needs of educational research differ greatly from the needs of the other behavioral disciplines.

The dangers of methodological transplant are not immediately obvious to most educators. Faced with an evaluation requirement, the educator turns to other behavioral scientists for an assessment scheme. Yet, because these behavioral scientists deal with specified conditions, their methods are usually applicable only under certain "closed-systems" assumptions which can deal with only a discrete number of selected variables. Although such models are appropriate for the study of some educational issues, most educational programs designed to produce changes require a more open, qualitative, analytic framework. In other words, most current methods of gathering, recording, and analyzing educational data are based on experimental models and require statistical-quantitative measurements, yet most educational encounters are nonexperimental ones (i.e., goal-specific operational field engagements), to which existent methodology yields little insight. The problem is further complicated because, although educators are told to control certain variables to see what happens to others, their substantive task is to manipulate as many variables as necessary to achieve multiple objectives which are often in conflict and of varying importance. As of now, there is no way of arraying these objectives and evaluating differential effects by manipulating restricted combinations of variables. Nor are there systematic procedures to assess the costs of accomplishing various effects. For these purposes, there is a growing tendency to turn to anthropology for guidance in developing sound program evaluation.

EVALUTION AS FIELD RESEARCH

It would be tempting to suggest that anthropology, either alone or in combination with other disciplines, provides a coherent set of methods and a theoretical base from which educational evaluation might develop a consistent conceptual framework and methodology. Such is not the case. In the first place, the task of examining, defining, and redefining the institutional setting in education should be the principal responsibility of the craft itself, and so it should not be assigned to some outside agency or group—no matter how willing it is to assume the task and how unwilling educators are to attempt it. Second, there *are* no existing preordained methods growing out of specific theories through which evaluators can approach the task of evaluation with assurance of success. There is no theoretical pattern for observation and analysis in any of the existing research strategies of the behavioral or social sciences which fits evaluation needs. Nothing emerges so clearly from "interdisciplinary" research ventures as the obvious fact that each discipline of the behavioral and social sciences has built its own conceptual framework and culture. Each is characterized by preferred ways of looking at and into the world. These preferences are not superficial: they characterize the kinds of questions asked, the ways they are asked, and the way in which answers are interpreted and presented.

In one respect, the educator's problems are comparable to those confronting the anthropologist. He, too, must observe, record, and analyze behavior in the field, not in a laboratory setting. Through the development of a conceptual model and correspondent methodology, anthropologists have achieved considerable precision in a natural environment. Over the last several years, this similarity of field strategy has led to increasing interest in what has come to be called the "anthropological method" or, more frequently, "anthropological approaches" to evaluation.

Although the phrase *anthropological approach* conjures up a nice image of evaluators as resident ethnographers describing the culture of the system they are studying, it is not only inaccurate but also dysfunctional because it perpetuates a number of growing misuses. In the first place, the anthropological approach has come to mean the use of participant observers without specifying anything about how participant observers are used. Participant observation is an important research style in anthropology (as it is in a number of other social sciences), but within that style it is necessary to develop skills in the use of technique. Most of the evaluations we have seen which propose to use participant observation usually stress observation to the exclusion of the participant role, and in many cases there is no clear definition of what is being observed or, more important, how it is to be observed, how it is to be recorded, and to what end this is all being done.

The use of untrained participant observers, who have no grounding in theory and who have not learned the difference between looking *at* and looking *for*, has created great problems in the field. School teachers and community residents have created their own "conspiracy" theory of evaluation. More and more, teachers and community people are viewing evaluation as a device for maintaining the system as it now exists. Evaluation is done, in this view, to inform educational decision-makers so that they can suppress any moves for change. When teachers are evaluated, like anyone else who is ever evaluated, they become uncomfortable. It is easy to assuage this discomfort by criticizing the evaluator. When participant observers who do not seem to know what they are doing appear on the scene, the teachers' attitude is exacerbated and criticism is fueled.

Whereas anthropological techniques appear simplistic at first (as one curriculum specialist told us, "I have been using the anthropological technique for years—I always visit my schools"), they are closely tied to conceptual frameworks which inform the methodology and are much more difficult to master than survey research or questionnaire approaches *because* they are much less structured. All of this is to underscore our major point—that field research techniques hold great potential for use in evaluation but that this should not be confused with anthropology. Fieldwork techniques are used broadly in anthropology as well as in sociology. In both cases they are related to theory and cannot be used apart from that theory. One of the major reasons field research techniques are so attractive to educational evaluators is that they allow for the gathering of vast amounts of descriptive data about schools, personnel, students, and community. Unfortunately, this very richness sometimes destroys the utility of the data because there is so much—quantitatively and qualitatively—that it cannot all be used. A conceptual framework within which to develop a strategy for field evaluation is also particularly pertinent for this reason.

COMBINING QUANTITATIVE AND QUALITATIVE APPROACHES

Given the complexity of current educational programs, particularly those which attempt innovation or remediation, it is necessary to collect a variety of behavioral, interactional, economic, and even political data for evaluation. Different methods can be used to collect and analyze these different types of data. The methodological problem involved, however, is to determine how best to combine these methods.

In selecting and combining research methods to construct an appropriate evaluation design, certain questions must be answered. At the very start, the purpose of the evaluation must be determined. Is the evaluation to provide information on program output, on the process of the program, or the cost-effective benefits? In addition, the evaluation design should reflect the role that the evaluation is to play in the decision-making process. This will determine the type of information feedback needed, the type of information to be collected, and the necessary phases for data collection. The researcher must also consider certain external constraints that are imposed on the research design. The scope of any research or evaluation design is constrained by the time and money available for the research and the problems of rapport and interaction between researcher and project participants. Such problems are usually severe in evaluation because of the nature of the enterprise. Finally, the technical issues of design, analysis, and measurement must be considered. This includes identifying pertinent questions about program impact and about what constitutes appropriate summary evidence in response to these questions (Bryk, 1978).

An array of research techniques is available to the evaluator from both the qualitative and the quantitative areas. The techniques range from methods requiring minimal interaction with a project (such as unobtrusive measures or archival review of records) to those involving moderate personal interaction with the site (such as with the use of scales, tests, and surveys) to those requiring active interaction with program participants (such as observation and interviews). In applying these methods to evaluation, the theoretical constraints as well as the methodological strengths or weaknesses of each technique must be considered. A technique may not fit a particular evaluation project because all standards of scientific inquiry cannot be satisfied.

As Weiss and Rein (1972) point out, traditional experimental designs are often not directly applicable to evaluation even though they are one of the most commonly used formats for evaluation. One of the reasons for the misfit between method and situation is the difficulty in selecting satisfactory criteria for assessing a program's impact. The goals and objectives of a program can change, especially when the aims of a program are broad. Moreover, it is difficult to develop operational measures of system change while still remaining sensitive to unanticipated change. Also, a program in progress cannot be controlled in evaluation as it would be in an experimental research situation. Finally, the "treatments" of a program are generally not standardized. This makes comparisons of program effectiveness difficult, and the variability and scope of goals make program gains less easily identifiable. As Bryk (1978: 39-40) noted, "The highly structured program whose primary objectives could be measured with some degree of accuracy tends to have more positive program effects than the 'open' programs whose full developmental perspective has so far eluded successful quantitative measurement."

Sieber (1973) suggests several ways that field observations and surveys can be used compatibly with each supplementing the design or methodological weaknesses of the other. Although Sieber (1973) explicitly considered only field observations and survey techniques, his thinking can be extended to other data collection methods, both qualitative and quantitative.

Sieber (1973) first illustrates how field methods can be of benefit to survey methods. Field methods can confirm survey data as well as provide the rationale for a survey design. Field methods can serve as background to a survey by providing familiarity with the setting being surveyed, by developing rapport with those being surveyed, and by performing exploratory work that is necessary for pretesting a survey. Field observation can add to the theoretical structure of survey analysis and can validate survey results. For example, field methods can be used to illustrate findings and to clarify ambiguous or provocative responses. Field methods can also supplement an experimental design. For instance, Bryk (1978: 51) argues that, to "pursue interaction questions . . . we must link the individual program effects that are emerging over time to the characteristics of the context. In statistical terms, we describe the full distribution of [the treatment effect], conjoint with multivariate data on individual program characteristics. The basic treatment/control group paradigm cannot provide this information." Finally field methods can be used to check the reliability of a survey or other quantitative technique.

Sieber (1973) also describes the way surveys contribute to field work. Surveys can help to inform the design of field work and add to the perspective for data collection so as, for example, to help the researcher obtain a representative sample and a holistic understanding of that sample. Survey methods also can be used to verify field interpretations and to cast new light on field observations, just as field methods are used to enlighten the analysis, of survey findings. Erickson (1977) points out, however, that the greatest benefit of quantitative methods is that they facilitate the generalizability of insights derived from qualitative data.

Denzin (1978: 292) suggests a more formal means of combining the methods, through the triangulation of research techniques. A researcher examines a problem (or problems) from as many different methodological perspectives as possible; "each method implies a different line of action towards reality—and hence each will reveal different aspects of it, much as a kaleidoscope, depending on the angle at which it is held, will reveal different colors and configurations of objects to the viewer."

According to Denzin, there are four sources of triangulation available to the researcher or, in this case, the evaluator: data (including time, space, and person); investigator (in which one uses several investigators for the same research); theoretical (using multiple rather than single perspectives on the same set of objectives); and methodological (either within a collection of instruments or among methods). "Within-method" triangulation is obtained when observational units are multidimensional or when a single survey makes use of different strategies. "Between-method" triangulation refers to the use of several data collection methods for the same data questions so that the flaws of one method can be compensated by the strengths of other methods.

Denzin (1978) suggests only one form of theoretical triangulation, where several theories are applied simultaneously to the same set of data. A different form of theoretical triangulation is possible in educational evaluation because programs often have more than one objective, each representing a particular thrust for achieving program impact. Thus, different theoretical models could conceivably be applied to different aspects of the same program. This might also lead to different or interrelated strategies of data collection.

A final means of combining these methods in evaluation is through the development of causal models based on field observations, as suggested by

Cooley (1978). Early attempts at quantification of qualitative data have been limited to descriptive statistics. (See Becker, 1969, for a discussion of another system for quantification of qualitative data.) But both Cooley (1978) and Fienberg (1977) note that qualitative research findings are capable of being modeled by inferential statistics, and they suggest that this is one way to improve the generalizability of qualitative findings.

Perhaps a couple of examples where qualitative and quantitative methods have been combined would help to fix these ideas. A recent major study of school violence made use of what might be called methodological "layering." The Safe School Study, conducted by the National Institute of Education, was designed in three phases. Phase I was a mail survey of 5,578 public schools in the United States; Phase II was an on-site questionnaire study of 851 of these schools in a representative sample; and Phase III was a series of in-depth case studies of ten schools scattered throughout the United States. The purpose of Phase III was to provide "real world" examples to enliven the largely statistical report from the other two phases. In this study, a reverse "layering" of methods might have been more useful. The comparative analyses of these ten case studies proved so powerful in identifying key variables that the earlier survey data were analytically reexamined, based upon the findings of Phase III.

In general, the proper sequence would be to begin with the ethnographic and clinical fieldwork and then to use the results of these initial studies to design survey instruments and to clarify the analyses of the survey findings. In this way ethnographic research can be used to describe the social field of interest and to identify the important variables, especially in the exploratory examination of social processes, which are poorly understood. This insures that research findings are "grounded," which endows them with a high site-specific validity though their intensive nature limits their generalizability. The survey portion of the study is then used to establish the generalizability of the ethnographically discovered findings.

A recent evaluation of an open classroom followed just such a procedure. This evaluation required an assessment of the cognitive, affective, attitudinal, and observational differences between the open classroom program and regular classroom programs in the district, and both program process and outcome were examined. Field observation was the first stage of the data collection process. Then interviews and questionnaires were constructed for relevant program participants to follow up on questions particularly concerning the identified program and evaluation objectives that developed during the observation phase. These interviews and questionnaires were also used to assess program-related problems and strengths, as well as to collect information about teacher practices and personal perceptions that could be generalized. These interviews and surveys were followed by yet another round of field observations to follow up on the findings of these efforts.

SUMMARY AND CONCLUSIONS

As indicated above, there is a growing tendency to turn toward qualitative methodologies in educational evaluation. In all cases that we have observed, there is an expectation that qualitative approaches will provide a research paradigm which attends to the sociocultural context of education and gives a real world quality to quantitative data.

We have suggested a number of reasons for this new interest in qualitative methods, one of the major reasons being that educational consumers are increasingly questioning the fit between the formal analytic models traditionally used by educational evaluators and the social reality of their schools. One result of the growing interest is that ethnographic approaches to evaluation are being used in a wide variety of school programs usually employing, often for periods of just a few days, "field researchers" with little training. True ethnography, in contrast, is characterized by years of in-depth study. We believe that the common approach using field researchers has done a disservice to education and is detrimental to the productive development of the qualitative measures needed for evaluation research.

Ethnographic descriptions of natural environments and ground-level reporting of what people say and do, rather than what they say they do have added a new empiricism to evaluative research. There are, however, a number of issues which still remain regarding the appropriateness of ethnography in evaluation. There is some question as to whether the preferred style in ethnography of the solitary field worker and the corresponding resistance to team research is appropriate to the current largescale, probelm-solving orientation of much of educational research and evaluation. Research administrators often are troubled by the individualistic style of anthropologists ("Our experience is that anthropologists not only prefer to work alone, they are actually disruptive if you mix them with other social scientists or educators") and the fact that team research is impossible in anthropology ("We seldom ask more than one anthropologist to work on a project because they seldom agree with each other"). Certainly some of the reservations of research administrators about the uses of anthropologists in educational research are realistic. Our own experience in team research convinces us of the truth of the old axiom that the problems encountered in team research increase numerically with the number of scientists involved. But the problems seem to increase geometrically when those scientists are anthropologists and exponentially when they are anthropologists mixed with other social scientists.

Another problem is that ethnographers tend to emphathize with those they study and in some cases seem almost to "go native." Personal involvement and immersion in the lives of the people studied leads ethnographers to become advocates (and there are numbers of anthropologists who maintain that this is appropriate). Thus, just as it is difficult to find ethnographies which are neutral in looking at tribal socieites versus colonialists, those of us who study urban American culture often tend to identify with the problems of the junkies, pimps, hookers, and inmates we work with while we, like them, see the "authorities" as oppressors. The early history of anthropological study of American schools reveals that ethnographers see the students as the oppressed and the teachers and administrators as somehow working to demean the students' natural learning styles. When we study teachers, it is the administrator who seems to be at fault. With the growing interest in ethnographic methods for evaluation in education, there is also growing uneasiness among project managers and administrators over what they consider the ethnographer's tendency to impose such ideological value judgments without fully understanding the problems from both sides. There are, of course, other reasons for looking holistically at schools and school districts. Advocacy is most effective in directing social change when all of the elements in a social system are related (see Nader, 1969).

Despite all this, we believe that qualitative approaches are essential to evaluation, particularly once we realize that participant observation is not the only qualitative technique. The theoretical and practical development of qualitative measures which can be integrated with quantitative approaches is essential. The history of educational innovation, and indeed of all recent social service programs, indicates clearly that when social action programs do not grow out of and reinform a body of theory they seldom survive long enough to produce any institutional change.

REFERENCES

BECKER, H. S. (1969) "Problems of inference and proof in participant observation," in G. McCall and J. C. Simmons (eds.) Issues in Participant Observation. Reading, MA: Addison-Wesley.

BRYK, A. (1978) "Evaluating program impact: a time to cast away stones, a time to gather stones together," in S. Anderson (ed.) Exploring Purposes and Dimensions. San Francisco: Jossey-Bass.

COOLEY, W. W. (1978) "Explanatory observational studies." Educational Researcher 7, 9.

DENZIN, N. K. (1978) The Research Act. New York: McGraw-Hill.

ERICKSON, F. (1977) "Some approaches to inquiry in school-community ethnography." Anthropology and Education Quarterly 7, 2.

FIENBERG, S. E. (1977) "The collection and analysis of ethnographic data in educational research." Anthropology and Education Quarterly 7, 2.

NADER, L. (1969) "Up the anthropologist—perspectives gained from studying up," in D. Hymes (ed.) Reinventing Anthropology. New York: Random House.

SIEBER, S. (1973) "The integration of fieldwork and survey methods." American Journal of Sociology 78: 133-159.

WEISS, R. and M. REIN (1972) "The evaluation of broad-aim programs: difficulties in experimental design and an alternative," pp. 236-249 in C. Weiss (ed.) Evaluating Action Programs. Boston: Allyn and Bacon.

EDITORS' NOTE

Some readers may find it somewhat strange that one of Howard Becker's papers on photography has been included in this volume. Photography is far from being a common technique of evaluation, and Becker, though a noted authority in qualitative research methods in the social sciences, is not noted for his contribution to evaluation. Indeed, the word evaluation does not appear in this paper in any of the senses traditionally used to characterize efforts to estimate changes due to projects or programs.

We have included Becker's paper for two reasons. First, photography can be of great use in evaluation. Investigative journalists have time and again demonstrated the effectiveness of dramatic photographs in drawing attention to, and in some way "epitomizing," particular social problems and the adequacy of strategies to alleviate them. One need only think of pictures of ambulance drivers refusing to carry obese actors who have feigned heart attacks on the third floor of a tenement, or photographs and films of disabled persons trying to negotiate high curbs, or the filmed news coverage of the Vietnam War. As a communication device, the camera has a great potential to set agenda and dramatize intervention attempts.

Photographs (and film) can also provide a more detailed and continual record of the processes and transitions that clients undergo in particular programs. In this way, photographs can provide a framework for understanding and classifying some of the important events that transpire during the course of a program. Of course, such usage is limited by expense (though time and person sampling techniques can reduce costs), and by any ways in which the camera's obtrusiveness might affect the behavior of the persons being photographed (though such problems are not unique to film).

The reference to obtrusiveness illustrates a second, and perhaps most important, reason for including Becker's paper. His discussion of the interpretation of photographs relies heavily on an epistemological premise that transcends the distinction between qualitative and quantitative methods. Becker argues that even with photographs the investigator has to think through which interpretations of the photograph are warranted and then try to use the image, knowledge of the surrounding circumstances, and any other relevant knowledge to rule out alternative interpretations for what the photograph seems to suggest. The framework is one of confirmation (i.e., determining which interpretations are confirmed) and disconfirmation (i.e., determining which plausible interpretations are ruled out). It is this succinct presentation of an epistemological framework common to quantitative and qualitative research that seems important to us.

Howard S. Becker

Northwestern University

6

DO PHOTOGRAPHS TELL THE TRUTH?

Do photographs tell the truth? Social scientists and photographers are equally concerned with the question, though they come to it by different routes. "Visual sociology" and "visual anthropology" are small but growing movements within those disciplines, and historians (Michael Lesy being the most obvious example) are toying with more imaginative and extensive use of photographs than had been customary. If we are going to use photographs as evidence for social science assertions, we need to know whether they can be trusted as evidence, whether and how they "tell the truth."

Photographers have a much more ambivalent concern with the truth of photographs, and often adopt a strategy that attempts to have it both ways, presenting photographs in a way that intimates, without quite saying, that they convey some important or essential truth about the matter they picture. But the photographers know perfectly well that the pictures represent a small and highly selected sample of the real world about which they are supposed to be conveying some truth. They know that their selection of times, places, and people, of distance and angle, of framing and tonality, have all combined to produce an effect quite different from the one a different selection from the same reality would produce. They worry that, because someone else could have photographed the same subject differently, they will be accused of bias. With that worry in mind, they think defensively and assert before they can be accused of it that their pictures are only a personal view, "just the way it looked to me," that any other personal view would be just as "valid." But they never really mean the disclaimers, either about their own pictures or about any other pictures that have any claim to documentary veracity.

You can easily prove to yourself the uselessness of the "it's-only-personal" disclaimer. Take some photograph that has a strong element of seeming to

---

Reprinted from Afterimage, *February 1978, 9-13. A few of the photographs have been omitted from the original.*

report on the truth about society or some portion thereof—the FSA photographs are good for the purpose, although they needn't be classics (I often use the photographs my students make). Now tell yourself, or some friends, or anyone who will listen, that you have just discovered that this picture was not made where it appears to have been made or where its caption says it was, or that the people in it are not who they seem to be or are not doing "naturally" what the picture shows them doing. I once upset a class by telling them that the pictures one student had made were phony in that, while they were photographed at O'Hare Field, every person in them was an extra he had hired and whose movements he had choreographed. The response to such an assertion is interesting. I have never known anyone to respond in any way other than to say, "It's not true!," even people who a moment earlier were asserting stoutly that the picture represented a personal view whose truth didn't matter. If we refuse to believe that a photograph does not have the warrant of reality we assumed it did, we must see that part of our response to it was a response to it as evidence of something about the real world and the photographer in it.

Not every photograph will produce such a response of course. Whole genres simply do not raise the issue of truth. No one knows or cares where a Uelsmann construction originated, and if Duane Michals uses models, so what? On the other hand, it would make a great deal of difference to us if we thought that even such obviously "personal" work as Diane Arbus's or Robert Frank's was not shot where it purports to have been or that the people who appear in those images were hired models; and the case is stronger when we think of photographs by W. Eugene Smith or the FSA photographers. Anyone whose response to photographs never includes this reaction need not read further.

Most of us, then, do worry about whether the pictures we make and look at are "true" and can be seen to be true by others who look at them. I want to suggest some ways of thinking about this question that are less confusing than the approaches we commonly take. In doing so, I will rely on some ideas more or less well-known to social scientists and will probably violate some photographic sensibilities, but that is the price of escaping the traps we get ourselves into.

What I will propose is not necessarily the best or the only or even a terribly important way of evaluating photographs, nor must all photographs be evaluated by the standards I will describe. But if truth is a factor in our response to a photograph then these standards are relevant to our understanding and judgment of it, and to our aesthetic experience of it as well.

WHAT'S TRUE?

A first clarification requires us to give up the question "Is it true?" In that simple form it is unanswerable, meaningless, and therefore foolish. Every photograph, because it begins with the light rays something emits hitting film, must in some obvious sense be true; and because it could always have been made differently than it was, it cannot be the whole truth and in that obvious sense is false.

To talk about the question more sensibly, we have to refine it. To begin, we can ask, "Is this photograph telling the truth about *what*?" Pictures can ordinarily contain enough information that we can use them to give us evidence about more than one topic. Are Brassai's pictures (in *The Secret of Paris of the 30's*) telling us the truth about Paris, or about Paris in the 1930s, or about the Parisian demi-monde, or about that sort of demimonde in general, or . . . ? Are Bill Owen's photographs (in *Suburbia*) telling the truth about suburbia in general, Livermore, Calif., in particular, about sex roles in modern America, about housekeeping practices, about American children, or . . .? So we must first specify what we are getting the truth about.

Even that is not enough. If we know the topic, we still don't know what is being asserted about it. We sometimes feel that the assertions a photograph makes—its "statement"—are so subtle and ineffable that they cannot be reduced to words. No doubt the entire statement cannot be reduced in that way. Much of it is made in a visual language that we don't have any workable rules for translating into words. Further, it contains so much material that reducing it to words would take more work than it is worth. Still, we do not usually feel that we can say nothing at all about the content of the picture. So we need a way of extracting from the image some verbal statements that will help us decide what, if anything, the picture is telling us the truth about, and what the truth is.

Here is a way to proceed. For any picture, ask yourself what question or questions it *might* be answering. Since the picture could answer many questions, we can decide what question we are interested in. The picture will, of course, suggest that some questions are likely to find answers in it. For instance, Owens's pictures of pantries and refrigerators clearly suggest that they will answer questions about what kinds of food the inhabitants of the houses store and presumably eat, while other pictures in *Suburbia* suggest that they will answer other questions about the housekeeping arrangements of these people. Walker Evans's photographs of sharecroppers' kitchens don't contain such detailed information about food and cannot be used to answer such questions; their content suggests that they will answer questions about the kind of household furnishings sharecroppers had to live with. In the same way, some of Brassai's photographs clearly answer questions about how Parisian whores did business, while Danny Lyon's pictures (in *The Bikeriders*) answer some of our questions about how members of motorcycle gangs spend their leisure time.

We needn't restrict ourselves to questions the photographs suggest. We can also use them to answer questions the photographer did not have in mind and that are not obviously suggested by the picture. Thus, Lesy (in *Real Life*)

Bill Owens, from *Suburbia*

Walker Evans, "Kitchen and Breezeway Wash Stand in Floyd Burrough's Cabin, Cotton Sharecropper, Hale Co., Ala., 1935"

uses photographs from a commercial studio to investigate how participants in the social life of Louisville in the '20s purposely altered reality, a question the pictures of Caulfield and Shook were meant to keep from awareness. We can thus avoid interminable, unresolvable, and irrelevant questions about the photographer's intent, for, whatever the intent, we can use the photograph to answer questions we want to raise and still not do violence to the work of artist-photographers.

In either case, we choose a question we think the photograph might enable us to answer. We may approach the photograph with the question already in mind or it may come to us as we inspect the image. Either way, we go over the image systematically to see what kind of answer it can give. We may find that it doesn't really answer the question very well, but will answer some other question more satisfactorily, leaving less margin for doubt. The job is to find a question and answer which fit each other, the answer being the answer for that question and vice versa.

The most obvious questions that photographs answer are the most specific. What did those people have on their pantry shelves? What kind of jackets did the members of Lyon's motorcycle gang wear? But we are only interested in such specific information if the subjects of the photograph are celebrities of some kind or intimates of ours, or if the photographs are to be used in a legal proceeding. Normally, we find photographs interesting because they answer questions about something larger than the immediate subject, and photographers usually give us to understand that their images have such broad meaning. Thus, Owens does not call his book *Livermore*, he calls it *Suburbia*, and in so doing intimates (presumably purposefully) that the photographs answer questions about the suburban way of life generally, not just about one suburb. If it were only about that one suburb, we would find the photographs less interesting; few people (other than those who live there) have a deep interest in Livermore, California. Books of documentary photographs often have titles that imply that kind of interesting generalization (think of *The Americans*, *American Photographs*, or *You Have Seen Their Faces*). But even without such help, we quickly jump to such generalizations, for without them the photographs would never command our attention at all.

So we usually inspect this kind of photograph with an eye to answering some general question about social arrangements or processes. The kinds of questions that concern us are often those social scientists ask. For instance, what are the main themes of the culture of this society? That is the kind of question Ruth Benedict raised in *Patterns of Culture* and *The Chrysanthemum and the Sword*, and I think it a fair way to characterize Robert Frank's book to say that *The Americans* is a kind of answer to such questions about the United States. The list of themes his book gives as an answer, if we should put that question to it, includes (and my list is not exhaustive) such themes as these:

(1) The automobile dominates American society. Americans revere their automobiles and practically live in them.

(2) they similarly revere the flag, or at least display it everywhere, in so many and such varied places as to devalue and degrade it.

(3) Religious symbolism is likewise omnipresent and thereby meaningless and degraded. Only among blacks is it a living force.

(4) Some males—white, upper middle class, middle-aged, or Westerners—are powerful, inspiring fear and deference. Older men are devalued, ignored, and badly treated, as are poor people and members of ethnic minorities.

(5) Women are powerless, and get by only on looks and an attachment to a powerful male.

This is not the place for a full-analysis of *The Americans*. But the nature of cultural themes is at least one order of question to which it gives answers.

Other photographic work characterizes the way of life of some social stratum, occupational group, or social area by detailing major forms of association among the group's members and placing them in relation to some set of environing forces. Danny Lyon's work does that. Other photographers answer questions that amount to some version of: can such things be? That is, they verify that certain phenomena have actually occurred or existed, so that we know that future talk and theorizing will have to take their existence into account. Insofar as Dian Arbus's published photographs tell us about something beyond herself, they serve that purpose, pointing to the existence of a population of freaks and weirdos ordinarily conveniently forgotten by more "normal" members of American society, a population ignored by both lay and professional theories of how the society works. Or take this question: would small-town American men, farmers and similar working-class people, perform cunnilingus in public on women who are total strangers to them? Most writers about American society would find that unlikely, but a few photographs in Susan Meiselas's *Carnival Strippers,* plust the supporting text, show us that they have, at least often enough for her to photograph it; on the testimony of her informants, the event is commonplace.

Further examples are unnecessary. We can read out of these photographs answers to such questions. The answers, both specific and general, that we find in the photograph can be taken as the propositions whose truth the photograph asserts. Thus, we no longer have to ask such unanswerable questions as "Is Smith's essay on the Spanish village a 'true' picture of life there?" Instead, we can ask specific questions about that life—do the villagers take religious rituals very seriously?—and use the material in the pictures to answer them. The first step in deciding whether pictures tell the truth, then, is to decide what truth they assert by seeing what answers we can extract from them to questions either we or they have suggested. (This way of looking at things emphasizes that pictures do not simply make assertions, but rather that we interact with them in order to arrive at conclusions —in short, that we play an active role in the process, as Dewey long ago argued and a host of other people have reiterated since.)

THREATS TO VALIDITY

Once we know what we think a picture asserts, or can be made to assert, we can ask: is the assertion true? Before I suggest a way of dealing with this problem I want to make a few preliminary remarks.

(1) The truth need not be the *whole* truth. It is irrelevant to criticize the assertion we have extracted from a picture because there is some other assertion it will also support, *unless* the two assertions are contradictory. Since pictures often contain a wealth of information, it is not surprising that more than one true thing can be said on the basis of a single image. When this happens, it only means that we are asking different questions, which deserve and get different answers.

(2) The truth will ordinarily not be verified by a single photographic image and usually not by any number of photographic images taken by themselves. Photographers and others have fallen into the habit of discussing the question of truth as though it had to be settled with reference to one picture—what can we assert for sure on the basis of this one picture? The answer is usually nothing at all. We generally decide important questions on the basis of an assessment of all kinds of evidence, balancing all the fragments of fact we can assemble to arrive at the best judgment we can make about a proposition. Those fragments will ordinarily include other photographs besides the one we are working with, *and* a variety of textual materials: documents, interviews, and so on.

(3) We can never be absolutely sure of the truth of an assertion. Our knowledge is always partial and therefore fallible; we may find a new piece of evidence tomorrow which will show us that the assertion we thought true is, after all, false. Thus, recent investigation of the circumstances of the making of many of the early photographs of American Indians shows that they are grossly inaccurate, because the photographers clothed and posed their subjects according to the way they thought Indians ought to look rather than investigating their lives sufficiently to be able to photograph them as they did look in ordinary life (see Scherer, 1975). This and similar

cases show how new information can shift our ideas about the validity of an assertion and thus the degree to which those ideas rest on more than the internal evidence deducible from one photograph.

(4) No single standard of proof is acceptable for all social groups and all purposes. Some groups are more skeptical than others, in part because of professional biases (i.e., psychologists are probably more skeptical than anthropologists) and in part depending on whose ox is being gored (proof of something that damages some cause of mine is going to have to be very convincing proof, much more so than in the opposite case). Further, we demand a higher standard of proof if we are going to base some important action on our conclusion. (One reason we are less skeptical about photographic materials may be that we seldom take any important action on their basis.)

With those qualifications, we can think about how to tell whether the assertion we have drawn from a photograph is true. The idea of *threats to the validity* of a proposition was first proposed and much elaborated by Donald Campbell, a psychologist and philosopher of science, and a number of his collaborators. The idea is simple enough. We decide whether a proposition is true (or, perhaps better, whether we ought to beleive it) by thinking explicitly of all the reasons we might have to doubt it, and then seeing whether the available evidence requires us to take those doubts seriously. If the evidence suggests that we need not entertain these doubts, that these threats to the validity of our idea are not sound, then we can accept the proposition as true.[1]

Campbell and others have listed a large number of threats to the validity of hypotheses or assertions. Many of them have special reference to the situation of the laboratory experiment; others are more generally applicable. I don't intend to go through their entire list, but rather to generate the beginnings of a similar list applicable to assertions based on photographic materials. We now have available many photographic monographs and essays which make some sort of statement about social life. Inspecting a variety of these works, we can see what doubts we have about them; generalizing those doubts, we can see what the general categories of threats to the validity of photographically derived assertions might be. (Campbell has revised his list several times since its first publication, and the list I will give is likewise provisional, to be extended on the basis of how it works in practice.) When we understand the threats to the validity of our assertion we can also see what kinds of material will deal with the threat. In short, we can compile a catalogue of problems and solutions. Here are some of them.

(1) The most obvious threat to the validity of a conclusion based on photographic evidence is the suspicion that the photograph was faked in

some way. It might have been retouched; Lesy shows some gross examples of filthy factories, worthy of Lewis Hine, magically turned into spacious sunlit, healthful places of work. The print might be composite of a number of negatives, showing people together who in fact never met. The people and things in the picture might have been specially arranged by the photographer, or by someone else (with or without the photographer's knowledge and consent), as in the case of Arthur Rothstein's "skull" picture. Rothstein photographed a bleached steer skull sitting on some parched earth in North Dakota. He had found the skull nearby and moved it around the square of bare dirt and some nearby grass, looking for the best light and angle. Republican politicians, in an effort to embarrass the Democrats and Franklin Roosevelt, charged that the picture was faked, that the skull had never actually been where Rothstein photographed it. They intimated that he carted the skull around with him looking for likely places to put it so as to dramatize the drought. What they objected to was the implied conclusion that the drought was so bad that cows were simply dying and rotting on the open range.[2]

Michael Lesy, from *Real Life: Louisville in the Twenties;* Courtesy of the University of Louisville Photographic Archives

Michael Lesy, from *Real Life: Louisville in the Twenties;* Courtesy of the University of Louisville Photographic Archives

The Rothstein story illustrates several points. Whether the picture is "true" depends on what conclusion we draw from it. If we take it as evidence that North Dakota cows were dying of thirst it is probably not true. If we take it as symbolizing a condition of drought, illustrating its severity, then it probably was true. The story also indicates what is required for a picture to be taken as unassailably "true." If we suspect that it has been covertly interfered with by someone so that it does not picture what would have been there without such interference, its value as evidence diminishes. Thus, we may not trust Irving Penn's pictures of Peruvian peasants (in *Worlds in a Small Room*) to tell us what kind of people they are, because Penn tells us that he arranged their poses himself, moving arms, legs, and torsos as he did with fashion models. Whatever we might conclude about peasant life and culture from the way they held themselves before the camera is now suspect, since it might only be Penn's idea of peasants that we see. Conversely, when a picture openly displays the visible signs of having been "doctored" (as in the images in Dawn Ades's *Photomontage*), we find no fault with it; no one is trying to fool us and we know that we must make any inferences with the doctoring in mind.

(2) The Rothstein story suggests a second threat to the validity of assertions based on photographs. Photography has an ambiguous status in relation to high art, and many photographers whose work is unabashedly commercial or journalistic also would like it to be taken as "artistic." They are encouraged in this by the overseers of the art photography world who periodically discover artistic merit in work of that kind, so that photojournalists like Cartier-Bresson and W. Eugene Smith are recognized as artists, their work hung in museums, bought and sold by dealers and collectors. No genre of photography seems immune to this. A strong move to take fashion photographs seriously has been launched and even aerial reconnaissance photographs made under Steichen's direction during World War I have received such treatment (see Sekula, 1975).

I don't want to debate the rights and wrongs of this practice here. Some of the people and photographs so ennobled deserve it; many do not. In any event, because photographers, whatever kind of work they are doing, may want to be recognized as artists, we sometimes suspect that they have made their pictures to fit into currently fashionable artistic styles, either technically and compositionally, or with respect to mood and subject matter. Thus, some years ago, Jones and Boruch mounted an exhibition of photographs of a dying California town: boarded up stores, deserted streets, a closed bank. The show received a respectful review from Margery Mann (1964) who, some months later, wrote an aggreived letter to the editor in which she announced that she had since been to that town and discovered that not a block away from the dying downtown was a brand new thriving downtown, with a new branch of the bank that had closed, two auto dealers, and other signs of prosperity. The photographers seemed to have succumbed to an "artisitc" desire for nostalgic stories of the death of the Old West. None of this is a criticism of the photographs or an assertion that they are untrue, only a statement that you cannot conclude from them that the town was dying; the photographers could be faulted only insofar as they had suggested that you could.

The desire to make "art" may, then, lead photographers to suppress details that interfere with their artistic conception, a conception that might be perfectly valid in its own right, but that unsuits the photographs for use as evidence for certain kinds of conclusions. Many social scientists have just this fear about photographs. It is a justified fear, but one relevant not only to photographs or to those photographs made with some artistic intention. Insofar as the artistic intention interferes with the photograph's evidentiary use, it does so by affecting the selection and presentation of details, so that some things are not shown, some details are emphasized at the expense of others and thus suggest relationships and conclusions without actually giving good cause for believing them, and by presenting details in such a way (through manipulation of lighting or the style of printing, for instance) as to suggest one mood rather than another. Since every way of making a photograph, whether for artistic purposes or for presentation as evidence in a courtroom, does all of these things, there is a problem, but it is one every user of photographs has. Further, every form of verbal material poses the same problems, for writing and oral testimony are likewise shaped with some audience in mind and must be interpreted and understood accordingly. So, knowing that the photographer had some artistic intentions does not invalidate the work as evidence; we can still decide that some conclusion is true. Knowing that, however, we will be alerted to certain threats to the validity of our assertions. These threats are not easily summed up, for they depend on whatever artistic conventions and fashions were current when the photograph was made. Knowing that, we can look especially for those kinds of sampling and presentational omissions or biases that might be associated with those conventions.

(3) We may suspect that the photographer has inadequately sampled the events that might have been photographed, failing to see all the things relevant to the question and answer we are interested in, or, having seen them, failing to photograph them. One of the chief problems here is access. Can we get access to the full range of relevant activities and, if we can, on what terms can that access be negotiated? What do we have to give in return? When we look at photographs as evidence, we want to know about access and terms. Photographers usually give us information on these points, either explicitly (as in Bruce Davidson's introduction to *East 100th Street* or Smith's lengthy text in *Minamata*) or implicitly, by the evidence of the pictures themselves. It's often said that a photograph records, among other things, the relation of the photographer to the people in the picture, whether that be intimate, friendly, hostile, or voueuristic. We can see, for instance, that Danny Lyon and Larry Clark (in *Tulsa*) must have been intimately involved with the people whose bike-riding and drug-taking they photographed, while Frank was a stranger to those he photographed; that Jill Freedman was a friendly acquaintance of the circus people she photographed, that Bill Owens knew some people in Livermore better than others but knew the area comprehensively, the way a reporter would. Part of our concern is always to know how much time the photographer spent; we trust the sample more if we know it was a long time. A week is one thing, a year or two is something else.

Getting permission or freedom to make photographs of people can profitably be viewed as a negotiation between them and the photographer. Each gives something and gets something. Most photographers have developed some way of handling this problem, but it is seldom discussed frankly or at length. What did the photographer trade for permission to do the work? For instance, I have spent two years photographing the people who provide emergency medical services for large outdoor rock concerts in the San Francisco Bay Area. The one rule I had to accept in order to get access with a camera to large parts of the operation was never to photograph, or use a photograph of, a patient's face; the reason is clear and understandable, and I accepted the prohibition as the price of doing the project at all. Nevertheless, people who see the work now cannot answer questions about what kinds of people the patients are or how they feel about the service they are getting, because of the rule I accepted during that negotiation.

A second problem is the photographer's theory. We don't photograph what is uninteresting to us or what has no meaning. What can have meaning and be interesting is a function of the theory we have about what we are investigating. We can usually get an idea of the photographer's theory by investigating both the pictures themselves and the accompanying text. We may decide that the theory has blinded the photographer to things we need to know to decide whether a particular assertion is true. We criticize here, insofar as we make a criticism, not the photographs but the theory or idea that lay behind their making. (See Becker, 1975.)

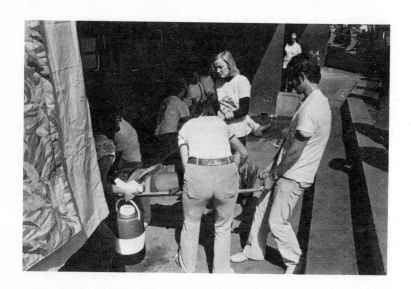

Howard Becker, from rock medicine series

In any event, an inadequate sample, however it came about, can lead us to feel a serious threat to the validity of the assertion we want to make based on the photographs.

(4) Finally, we may suspect that some form of censorship has prevented us from seeing all the pictures we might have seen, and that the ones that have been withheld would have changed our view substantially and perhaps even altered our conclusions. Censorship may be imposed by the state or some subdivision thereof, by a general cultural atmosphere that makes certain photographs unseemly or distasteful, or by photographers themselves out of some personal or political conviction.

Contemporary standards have loosened up so much with respect to "moral" issues that we now see photographs that would not have been made public only a few years ago. A striking example of this is Brassai's new book, which includes his already famous photographs of Paris plus many other photographs made at the same time but presumably considered too raunchy for public exhibition or distribution then, but not now. So we now see the gay bars we didn't see before, the whores and their customers in private, and so on. None of this contradicts what we saw before; it extends and amplifies it just as we might have imagined, without being quite sure we were right, even though our worldly wisdom told us we probably were.

But because we now see these pictures doesn't mean that we don't still have to consider the possibility of censorship. In particular, keep in mind that sex is only one topic which may be censored. There are many others. Anything people don't want known about, and there are millions of such things, may be censored if those who want the matter covered up have the power to do it. In fact, preventing things from being made public is one element of the practice of public relations, and businesses and communities, in particular, often try to keep "unfavorable" material, including photographs, from being made public. Though carried on by private parties rather than the government, and not the result of some general cultural standard, this too has the effect of limiting what we see.

The photographer may similarly limit what we see. In this case, of course, there is a nicer name and a rationale for what is done. We often speak of editing, meaning the weeding out of a small pile of superior pictures from the larger mass of all the photographs. It is unlikely that we would want to see all that material, although it is not, for instance, ridiculous to suggest that proof sheets might be available for independent checking—everyone has found it extremely interesting to see the full range of negatives Walker Evans produced for the FSA. We will frequently find that seeing the larger body of work will not change our ability to make various assertions or the warrant for those assertions. But it might, and we might want to know about that before accepting the answer to some question.

Photographers may also censor their work for reasons of ideology or ethics, as I have done with the faces of rock medicine patients. Without being required to by circumstances, they may decide that they don't wish to show everything, that some things are no one's business or disrespectful to the people being photographed. It is instructive to compare the work of Bill Owens and Roslyn Banish in this respect. Banish (in *City Families*) has treated a somewhat similar subject matter to that Owens worked with (the only difference being that she is interested in the domestic life of city dwellers instead of suburbanites) in a quite different way. Instead of Owens's "candid snapshots," with the one short, snappy statement by the subject appended, she made formal family portraits, to which are appended lengthy interviews, filled with details about the families' lives and aspirations. The much more respectful photographs present the families in a dignified, sober way that emphasizes their respectability and dignity. Owens does not let his people stay so buttoned up; he persuaded them to show a less dignified, more comic side to the camera, and at the same time has not allowed them to speak for themselves at such length. Owens's

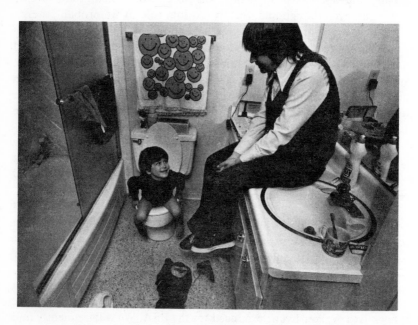

Bill Owens, "Andrew Doesn't Like To Go to the Bathroom Alone," from *Suburbia*

Roslyn Banish, photograph of Entwistle family, from *City Families* (Pantheon, 1976)

photographs give us much more information about a variety of topics (what goes on behind the neat walls of these suburban cottages? Disorder, drinking, bad taste, sloth, and mess?) and much less about a variety of other topics (hopes, dreams, and aspirations). If I had my choice of a basis for understanding families-in-an-environment, I'd like to have both; I can answer more questions more completely from the combination than with either one taken alone. I don't know if it's fair to call Banish's respectful photographic editing or Owens's severe editing of his subjects' words censorship; probably not, but the effect is the same and in each case means that we can have less confidence in the conclusions we draw from the material presented than we might otherwise have.

There will always be reasons good enough for some people not to present all the material they might, whether the reasons are matters of ethics, politics, or just good taste. In seeing what we can conclude, what questions we can answer plausibly, we must take into account whatever we know or suspect about the degree to which this kind of selection occurred. We must recognize that others will regard whatever signs of such selection they discover as weaknesses in the argument we are presenting, and thus we will want to avoid such biases, hide their signs or explain what they are and why they are present.

One final point. Insofar as we take some particular way of doing things as evidence that a suspected threat to the validity of some answer we are drawing from a photograph is not operating, we must be watchful for the possibility that the sign of authenticity itself has been faked. Many photographers now print their photographs with a heavy black line around the border of the print. Among other things, the line indicates that the negative has not been cropped, that all its evidence has been openly and honestly presented to us. But, of course, black lines can be made around parts of a negative. And, more to the point, the device obscures a more serious threat: any ordinarily skillful photographer can frame an image so as to leave out the unwanted details a less skillful person would have had to crop.

CONCLUSION

To repeat, my purpose here has been to begin the discussion, not to conclude it. The list of threats is sketchy, the suggestions for means of dealing with them hardly even suggestive. The way to proceed, I think, is to continue to investigate successful practice—works that convince and succeed in overcoming doubt—in both social science and photography, learning from and generalizing from experiences in both areas.

NOTES

1. The original statement of the approach is Campbell and Stanley (1966). Some important revisions are suggested in Campbell (1969).
2. The story is told in Hurley (1972: 86-92).

REFERENCES

BECKER, H. S. (1975) "Photography and sociology." Afterimage (May/June).
CAMPBELL, D. T. (1969) "Prospective: artifact and control," in R. Rosenthal and R. L. Rosnow (eds.) Artifact in Behavioral Research. New York: Academic Press.
——— and J. C. STANLEY (1966) Experimental and Quasi-Experimental Designs for Research. Chicago: Rand McNally.
HURLEY, F. J. (1972) Portrait of a Decade. Baton Rouge: Louisiana State University Press.

MANN, M. (1964) Review. Artforum (May).
——— (1964) Letter. Artforum (September).
SCHERER, J. C. (1975) "You can't believe your eyes: inaccuracies in photographs of North American Indians." Studies in the Anthropology of Visual Communication 2: 67-86.
SEKULA, A. (1975) "The instrumental image: Steichen at war." Artforum (December): 26-35.

Michael S. Knapp
Stanford University

7

ETHNOGRAPHIC CONTRIBUTIONS
TO EVALUATION RESEARCH
The Experimental Schools Program Evaluation
and Some Alternatives

In recent years, evaluation research studies have begun to make use of ethnographic field work as one component in multidisciplinary team research efforts. One prominent example of this —evaluative research directed at the federally-funded Experimental Schools Program—provides a detailed record of the problems and possibilities of ethnographic research.

Given a heavy investment in fieldwork, a long time frame, and a study design calling for an approximation of conventional ethnographic research, the ES studies are an excellent starting point for a discussion of what ethnography can—and cannot—offer evaluation research. This paper will synthesize the published commentary of those involved in this set of studies, some two dozen articles and one book which have emerged over the past five years in the literatures of applied anthropology, evaluation, and organizational change. As the experience of those involved amply demonstrates, fundamental issues are raised by the use of ethnography in evaluation research which are more difficult to resolve the more the ethnographic component resembles conventional ethnographic practice. The difficulties are not impossible to surmount, but can be resolved only at great cost and with modifications to conventional ethnographic practice.

The task which ES researchers faced represents only one particular program, policy context, evaluative purpose, and level of research

AUTHOR'S NOTE: *I acknowledge the helpful comments made by Lee J. Cronbach, Woodrow W. Clark, Robert E. Herriott, Mitchell D. McCorcle, and Robert B. Textor on earlier versions of this chapter.*

investment. Other applications of ethnography to evaluation research are possible, each with special advantages and disadvantages and each departing in varying degrees from conventional ethnographic work. Selected reports of these alternatives will be discussed, in hopes of broadening the debate initiated by the ES studies and increasing the range of ethnographic contributions to evaluation research.

Ethnographic Research

To clarify terminology, ethnographic research refers to the descriptive fieldwork activity of cultural anthropologists and many qualitative sociologists. The basic elements of ethnographic research include: (a) an initially exploratory and open-ended approach to the research problem; (b) intensive involvement of the researcher in the social setting being studied, as observer and in varying degrees as a participant; (c) the use of multiple intensive research techniques, with emphasis on participant observation and key informant interviewing; (d) an explicit attempt to understand events in terms of meanings held by those in the social setting; (e) an interpretive framework which emphasizes the important role of context in determining behavior and the "holistic" or "ecological" interrelationship of behavior and events within a functional system;[1] (f) a research product in written form—an "ethnography"—which interprets events along lines suggested above and describes the setting in sufficiently vivid detail so that the reader "knows what it feels like to be there." While sufficient for purposes of this paper, this list of elements does not do justice to the complexities of ethnographic research as described more completely by anthropologists (e.g., Berreman, 1968; Wax, 1971), qualitative sociologists (e.g., McCall and Simmons, 1969; Filstead, 1970), or educational ethnographers (e.g., Wolcott, 1975; Wilson, 1977a).

ETHNOGRAPHIC EVALUATION RESEARCH IN THE EXPERIMENTAL SCHOOLS STUDIES

The "program" towards which ES evaluation research was directed comprised several subprograms, each consisting of independent responses to a general directive for "comprehensive and longterm change" in established educational systems. In selected school districts across the country, locally developed plans for innovation in staffing, curriculum, teacher preparation, and organization were supported by federal funds over three to five years. The sponsoring agency acted as a "partner" in the change effort by supplying funds, advice, and limited technical assistance (see Herriott, 1979a: 51). Local realizations of the program mandate varied in scope, degree of alteration in existing practice and organization, and extent of implementation.

The ES Program as a whole took place in a national policy context marked by considerable turbulence from the time of the program's inception in 1972 until the present. Initially a major Nixonian initiative at educational reform, the program weathered several changes of the guard in the White House, an awkward shift in sponsorship from OE to NIE, and several difficult years within NIE, as the agency fought off attacks from Congress and other constituencies (Herriott, 1979a). The program was guided by different management at various times in its life history, each with different expectations of it.

ES Evaluation Research and Its Ethnographic Component

The overall ES evaluation research strategy called for an interdisciplinary effort to gather data of two basic sorts. First, descriptive cases studies "documented" the progress of the program at each site, in the form of site histories and ethnographic accounts. Second, a battery of survey and psychometric instruments collected common "evaluative" information across all sites, so as to assess change in pupils, school organization, and community.

Some members of the evaluation community—and some participants in the ES studies—would draw distinctions between the "evaluation" and "documentation" components and would insist that ethnographic fieldwork was only a part of the latter and had no important evaluative role. This paper assumes, however, that it is more productive to treat both components as an integrated program of "evaluative research," each part of which was able to influence the other as well as policy matters or future decisions affecting the program.

Seven different research firms participated in the evaluation research effort, each conducting a study of one of the ES subprograms. Accounts of two of these studies have reported extensive ethnographic components, each organized somewhat differently (Herriott, 1977; Everhart, 1975, 1976). In one case—Project Rural, which has been most prominently discussed in the literature—one ethnographically trained fieldworker resided at each of ten school districts for long periods of time (ranging from three to five years depending on the site).[2] The fieldworker's time was divided roughly in half between the production of case studies and the gathering of cross-site data. The rest of the evaluation team, composed of personnel with psychological and sociological backgrounds, stayed at the research firm and was responsible for research and instrument design as well as for the extensive analyses performed on data relayed back from the field. The division of labor seemed to make sense, given the remote location and dispersion of the school sites.

In the second case, reported by Everhart (1975, 1976), the fieldworker was part of an interdisciplinary team located at the schools site and was apparently able to devote a larger portion of time to ethnographic work. Because of proximity to the other members of the team, the fieldworker interacted on a continuing basis with other elements of the overall research effort. In both cases, fieldworkers produced a case study approximating a traditional ethnography, in addition to doing other tasks not usually performed by ethnographers.

The rationale for the inclusion of a formal ethnographic component of either type seems eminently sensible. Given the expected variation from site to site, the multifaceted nature of the changes the program was supposed to promote, and the obvious inseparability of local program realization from its immediate context, the choice of putting many resources into an ethnographic component was reasonable. The training of ethnographers, not to mention their socialization to work in remote areas, seemed ideally suited for the task.

Convincing as this rationale was—and is—it paid insufficient attention to the difficult issues raised by the combination of formal ethnography and evaluation research. These issues are dramatically illustrated by the experiences of those involved in the ES studies, both at the fieldworkers' level and at that of the research coordinator or program sponsor.

ISSUES EMERGING OUT OF
THE ES EVALUATION RESEARCH EXPERIENCE

1. PROBLEM DEFINITION

Conventional ethnography comes from a tradition emphasizing an initially open-ended and exploratory approach to the definition of the research problem (Wolcott, 1975: 113). But in the context of evaluation research, sponsors tend to have more targeted concerns at the outset: a specific program or policy, a particular group of people, a range of variables believed to be "policy relevant," and a set of questions typically including: Did the program work? Were objectives achieved? Were program components implemented as planned?

Despite the latitude given them in the ES studies, the fieldworkers found themselves caught in the middle between the definitions of the research problem imposed by the sponsor or its constituencies and their own proclivity to "discover what the problem is" through developing sensitivity to the research setting and its occupants. One commented on resisting pressure by study coordinators to investigate specific program effects in a way that would have greatly narrowed the focus of ethnographic work. The fieldworker reported receiving "severe criticism from our own parent organization for not looking solely at outcome variables, and for not basing our entire five-year effort on how every action had implications for project objectives . . . we argued [instead] that the project had to be examined in its context, that is, as a 'transplant' of sorts into the living organism of the school district" (Everhart, 1976: 20).

Considerable efforts were made in Project Rural to preserve the fieldworkers' freedom to define a suitable theme for their ethnographic work, and guarantees to this effect were eventually worked into contracting arrangements (Fitzsimmons, 1975: 189). Still, the fieldworkers' other responsibility as gatherers of cross-site data complicated the process of defining a research problem. The nature of items in the cross-site instruments, for example, gave an impression to school site personnel of what the study's "real" concerns were, thereby restricting the freedom of fieldworkers to tackle a problem as they saw fit. One cited an example of gathering survey information on the condition of a clergyman's church, which elicited a negative reaction from the respondent, with the net result that the research firm "gained their information but it was not possible for me to return to this sector of the community relying on unobtrusive information, limited participation, or indirect interviewing" (Clinton, 1975: 199). In this instance, not only was research problem definition potentially affected, but also the crucial element of rapport with informants.

2. RAPPORT AND THE PROGRAM-SPONSOR RELATIONSHIP

Establishing a workable long-term fieldwork role is difficult enough for any ethnographer, but it becomes even more complicated in the evaluation research situation because of the nature of the relationships between parties. Given the nature of the information gathered by the researcher and the manner in which it is collected, it is difficult for an ethnographic evaluator to avoid a tremendous amount of suspicion from potential informants.

Ethnographic fieldworkers always face a delicate problem of legitimizing their information-gathering activity. They must establish and maintain rapport with the group they are studying. The information they gather is detailed, personal, and comes only through continued contact with people in the social setting under study. In a very real sense the fieldworker *is* the primary research instrument (Wolcott, 1975: 115). A new kind of role must be created—that of the "insider-outsider" (Pelto and Pelto, 1978: 189)—and people in the social setting must be persuaded that this role is acceptable. This research approach has been developed primarily in settings where a specific program was not the focus of study and where the researcher's institutional affiliation bore no obvious relationship to program funding sources. Furthermore, ethnographic fieldworkers have always had a "way out": given persistent adverse reactions, they could move to another site.

Evaluation researchers of any methodological persuasion find themselves in a triangular relationship involving themselves, program personnel, and program sponsors (who are usually evaluation sponsors, as well). The evaluator's position is organizationally precarious—an ambiguous "in-between" role which has been extensively commented on in the evaluation literature (e.g., Caro, 1971). Fieldworkers in the ES studies found themselves in just such a role, in between program personnel and sponsoring agency personnel. To complicate matters, the fieldworkers were only part of a large evaluation research effort, and so had to deal with other members of the research team as well.

The organizational ambiguity of the evaluator's role and the usual problems associated with rapport-building combined to create an especially difficult situation for the ES fieldworkers. Despite assurances to the contrary, information collected by the ethnographers was perceived by school site personnel as influencing the flow of federal funds to the school district. Fieldworkers were repeatedly treated as "government spies," which made the establishment of adequate rapport problematic and in some cases impossible (Herriott, 1977: 110). Also, in some cases, the inconsistent signals received by school site people from program officers of the sponsoring agency further complicated matters (see Everhart, 1975: 208-209). Fieldworkers were seen as the primary government "representative" on the scene; as a consequence, they spent inordinate amounts of time building relationships so that even a modicum of ethnographic work could be done.

The consequence of an inability to establish an adequate level of rapport with key members of the group under study go beyond fieldworker discomfort. In one case, a fieldworker's stay in the field was cut short prematurely because of continuing poor relations with site personnel (Herriott, 1977: 111). For others, access to data was either denied or the data distorted as informants tried to manipulate the flow of information to the fieldworker (Clinton, 1975: 201).

In short, the very nature of the conventional ethnographic approach— long immersion in the field setting and continuing intimate contact with informants—means that fieldworkers face a rapport-building task far greater than that of the evaluator periodically visiting sites to collect survey or test data. It is to the credit of the ES ethnographers that they were able to create an adequate level of confidence among their informants, as some have reported doing (e.g., Colfer, 1976: 38), but they did so at considerable cost in time and energy that might otherwise have been devoted to gathering data.

3. CONFIDENTIALITY AND THE POTENTIAL CONSEQUENCES OF INFORMATION

Any ethnographer faces difficult questions about the ownership and disposition of the reams of fieldwork data generated by field research. The issue is salient at several stages in the fieldwork process. First, as data is being collected, the ethnographer must decide whether to divulge any of it, a temptation which becomes greater the more he participates in program activities or provides feedback to program personnel. Second, as data is being analyzed and reported, the ethnographer must decide how much to protect the anonymity of sources, no easy matter in a research tradition which holds that "good" ethnographic reporting contains substantial amounts of primary data in the form of quotes, critical incidents, and the like (Wolcott, 1975: 124). At either stage, the issue is the same: Does the researcher have the right to reveal information, much of it private and personal, which implicates particular people and may have negative consequences for them? The answer to the question is not obvious and depends a good deal on the specific case. Most anthropologists agree on the following guideline: Disguise the identity of specific actors or places as much as is practical, and avoid presenting data that could bring harm to individuals.[3]

Any form of evaluation research raises this same kind of issue, but the dilemmas are most acute in the case of ethnographic fieldwork, as the ES case amply demonstrates. To begin with, a particular school site with particular people was the focus of each ES fieldworker's case account. As one put it, "Anonymity of research population is a dead issue in this case ... [as] is disguising major players. ... A rural school system contains a small number of teachers, fewer building administrators . . . and only one superintendant." (Clinton, 1975: 200). Furthermore, it was not possible to create averages of individual's performance, nor is that the kind of data ethnography is designed to yield. Reporting after the sound and fury are over—for example, after federal funding ends—represents a partial solution, assuming that audiences are ready to listen to findings at that time. But in the ES case, interim products were demanded of the fieldworkers to assure the sponsoring agency that work was progressing satisfactorily and to give it information to protect itself from hostile groups in Washington. The sponsor's suggestion that interim reports be made in secret only compounded the ethical problem facing fieldworkers, as one reported (Colfer, 1976). Every solution in this case represented some violation of initial assurances of confidentiality. Recognizing the same problem, another fieldworker suggested alternative interim products which would have caused little difficulty, such as reports dealing with non-programmatic concerns or the historical antecedents of the school system under study (Burns, 1976: 32). In principle, these solutions are possible, but they beg the question: The sponsor is most interested in knowing about the targeted program. And especially at the federal level, there is a high likelihood that the sponsoring agency will have some pressing political need for information about the program before a longterm evaluation research study is completed.

4. THE ETHNOGRAPHIC REPORT AND THE IDENTIFICATION OF POLICY VARIABLES

Conventional ethnographic research produces an "ethnography," a dense, vivid description and analysis of the social setting being studied, typically several hundred pages long or more. Its purpose is to convey in detail the workings of an intricate social system or some aspect of one. It takes a long time to do an adequate job—some writers suggest that an equal amount of time must be devoted to the writing of an ethnography as is devoted to the gathering of field data (Wolcott, 1975: 118).

For several reasons, the ethnographic report itself tends to fall short of providing the specific implications for policy or administrative action which are the typical end product of evaluation research. For one thing, the ethnography is not likely to single out the program as a distinct or particularly forceful determinant of events in the social setting being studied. Rather, the school site and its program tend to be interpreted in functional terms, as parts of larger self-maintaining systems (see Everhart, 1976: 21). Similarly, the ethnography may direct attention away from those variables which can be manipulated in a politically viable way by those with authority to allocate program resources. One fieldworker in the ES case summarized his perception of what policymakers want: "Policy-makers want quick and simple information on a focused problem in order to provide information on variables that can survive the administrative-legislative process" (Everhart, 1976: 20).

Although the case may be overstated, a clear tension exists between the typical ethnographic report and informational needs of many key people in the policy process. As observed by one member of the sponsoring agency, the fractionation of issues in the policy process, the search for short-term issues, and the sheer number of players in the game, all exert pressure for discrete, politically negotiable policy variables (Mulhauser, 1975: 313). Such variables tend to be difficult to find in most ethnographic reporting which follows the traditions of the anthropological discipline. Often, the better the ethnography, the less responsive it is to the immediate political needs of the relevant policy community.

But the dilemma can be viewed either as a "mismatch" or a "creative tension." The ES case provides an example of the way the tension may be productively managed. In principle, it is possible to synthesize case study findings in such a way that they yield policy implications. Exactly this was done in Project Rural (Herriott and Gross, 1979). Reduced case study accounts describing the process of program implementation at five sites were read and interpreted by the coordinators of research, as well as a panel of educators, who discussed the policy implications of the case studies. To take one example, a reviewer of the Project Rural accounts recommended (among other things) that sponsoring program agencies in the future pay special attention to the problem of program officer turnover, set up more equal negotiating relationships with local programs, and reorient the "management" emphasis of federal technical assistance toward one dealing more explicitly with the political nature of program implementation at the school site (Gideonse, 1979: 319-327). These recommendations were based on substantial evidence in the case studies of continuing poor relationships between local personnel and federal program officers, combined with some evidence that the interaction could be improved with better trained, more stable program officers. To the extent that recommendations such as these find an audience in Washington—and accurately distill the events described by the fieldworkers—the ethnographic work seems to have served a useful purpose.

It is also possible over the long term for ethnographic reports to help reshape thinking in Washington about what is relevant to policy formation, what variables can and should be manipulated. At the least, ethnographies may communicate a needed negative message regarding certain types of programs—such as, "you can't get there from here!" But it is too soon to assess the contribution of ES ethnographic reports to this kind of reframing of policy variables.

5. GENERALIZABILITY AND THE SINGLE CASE.

Ethnographic research is an ideographic approach to the study of social phenomena: it strives to capture the complexities of the single case. Within that case, the ethnography describes "general" patterns, that is, regularities within the social system. Patterns observed or extracted from the testimony of a few key informants are "generalized" by an inductive logic to all those sharing the same culture and participating in the same kinds of activities. Ultimately, ethnographic work contributes to the search for larger cross-cultural regularities in human behavior, as different ethnographic accounts are compared and contrasted, but this work falls more often to the ethnologist than to the ethnographer.

In the ES studies, the ethnographic component was arranged to contribute intensive descriptions of single cases, each done by one fieldworker. The use of multiple sites—as in Project Rural —made it possible for research coordinators, sponsoring agency, or others to look for more general patterns of response to the program. Finally, nonethnographic components were explicitly comparative: they sought standardized information across all sites, so as to generate a more general picture of program effects on pupils, school organization, and local community.

The ethnographic component in ES evaluation research dramatizes a fundamental tension: the ideographic focus and inductive logic of ethnographic research does not match the penchant of sponsors for generalizable results based on nomothetic research knowledge and deductive logic. The sponsoring agency wanted to know whether the ES program concept could be exported to other sites. In other words, would the ES program —or some form of it—lead to predictable positive outcomes in other settings? Such predictions typically rest on the notion of statistical generalizability, which plays a central role in nomothetic research modes, and has a special kind of political credibility these days to most members of the policy-making community. One member of the agency sponsoring the ES Program and its evaluation research has argued that ethnographies were not useful because (among other things) they "describe one or a handful of a class of places or institutions, rather than comparing a large number" (Mulhauser, 1975: 314).

More important perhaps than the small number of school sites which they describe, the ethnographies' focus on the fine detail of events at each site makes it hard to know the basis for asserting that the ES Program had a "general" effect. At one of the Project Rural sites, for example, the original project goals were gradually adapted and incorporated into the curriculum; at the same time the sponsoring agency made little effort to rigidly manage the program (Donnelly, 1979). At another site, administrative commitment to project goals steadily declined, a series of unrelated program components were unevenly implemented, and the sponsoring agency made active efforts to shape the local program plan (Messerschmidt, 1979). Although the juxtaposition of these patterns raises interesting questions concerning, for example, the effect of active intervention by the sponsor, the comparison is not constrained enough to permit the kind of general finding to which many policy-makers today tend to pay heed.

But the line of argument advanced here probably misrepresents the kind of generalizability which is called for in evaluation research. The real issue for those participating in program-relevant policy or administrative action is this: They want evidence that they can confidently extrapolate to situations beyond the logical reach of *any* generalized findings. In other words, there is still a leap of faith required in moving from any statistically based generalization to new program applications (see Cronbach, 1978: 301-355). Policy-makers are more likely to make that leap of faith where the extrapolation appears plausible and where it appears politically convincing to their most important constituencies.

Seen in this light, ES ethnographies may permit—or assist—members of the policy community to make more confident extrapolations of ES findings to new applications of the ES Program model or to similar ventures. The very complexity of the case findings, taken either singly or together, and the vividness of case descriptions may suggest plausible extrapolations to situations which the original program designers never considered. And, for better or worse, excerpted portions of the case accounts have considerable potential to persuade audiences through their capacity to "take the reader there." However, the point remains hypothetical at this stage. New applications of ES findings have yet to be discussed in the published literature. When the ES studies are finally completed and released to various audiences, some of their potential for generating convincingly "generalizable" knowledge about federally-stimulated comprehensive change processes may be realized.

6. COSTS: FUNDS, TIME, POLITICAL RESOURCES

Conventional ethnographic research is labor intensive and, in a sense, redundant: it covers and recovers the same ground for long periods of time in search of clues to subtle features of the social system. It is an expensive way of doing research, if cost is measured in terms of the time and attention required of highly trained professional people. Also, by virtue of its focus on a single and often small social setting, its "cost per unit studied" is especially high.

In the context of evaluation research, the problem is compounded as a larger series of costs becomes involved in the mounting of a research effort. Not only are funds scarce, but so are political resources and time. Those who sponsor evaluation research and those who use its products maneuver in a shifting field of political interests, bounded by time constraints which are often unpredictable. The ES studies had the luxury of bountiful resources at the outset: millions of dollars for research, a five-year time frame, and a favorable configuration of political events. But the political field changed rapidly and drastically, in a way that affected the supply of all three kinds of resources. The sponsoring agency and the ES program within it found themselves politically challenged; their response could have affected the survival of the entire project.

The ethnographic component was least able to respond to this threat, in large part because its findings were not easily displayed in midstream. Reams of fieldnotes are not easy to synthesize on short notice; much of their content is sensitive information. Overt efforts by fieldworkers to respond to accountability demands risked upsetting the delicate relationships which had been built—with considerable difficulty—at the schoolsite. In Project Rural, fieldworkers located in remote field settings were not in a position to respond quickly and persistently to pressures which threatened the project. Not surprisingly, ethnographic work was considerably curtailed: in some cases fieldwork originally projected for five years was shortened to three (e.g., Burns, 1976: 31). However, it is to the credit of fieldworkers and research coordinators that the ethnographic work was maintained as much as it was in the ES studies.

The ultimate cost-benefit question—whether the ES ethnographic components were worth the investment—is hard to answer at this point. Clearly, the components were maintained at considerable cost. The long-range value of the investment will only begin to be evident, if it can be detected at all, with the appearance of synthetic efforts such as that by Herriott and Gross (1979) and with the filtering of research summaries through the policy process.

ALTERNATIVE CONTRIBUTIONS OF ETHNOGRAPHY TO EVALUATION RESEARCH

The discussion so far has been oriented toward one kind of evaluation research situation—that of the large-scale federal demonstration project—and to one instance of this category of studies. In that context, the fundamental tensions involved in the definition of the research problem, the building of rapport, and the maintenance of confidentiality make ethnographic fieldwork especially problematic. One step removed from the field, the complexity of ethnographic reporting and its different basis for generalizability make its input into the policy process uncertain. The overall costs of a full-blown ethnographic component are also especially high, not only because of the intensive nature of fieldwork but also because of its political vulnerability and special time demands.

A broader understanding of the issues and the alternative ways in which ethnography can contribute to evaluation research requires experimenting in other evaluative contexts with different purposes, time frames, and levels of research investment. Accounts of such experiments are beginning to emerge in the literature, though so far with less visibility than discussions of the ES case.

Three themes appear in the literature. First, it is possible to do more of the same: that is, to incorporate large-scale ethnographic components similar to that of the ES studies into other federally-sponsored evaluation research ventures. Second, ethnographic evaluation can be especially useful, when the primary audience of the study is the program itself—that is, where ethnographic fieldwork is put to more formative ends. Third, more limited ethnographic components may be built into evaluation research designs to document program implementation, to demonstrate plausible connections between certain policy variables, or to assist in the development of sensitive research instruments.

Refining the Experimental Schools Model

As more large federal studies build in the ethnographic component similar to that used in Experimental Schools research, it is possible that better solutions to the previously discussed problems will be found. One NIE-sponsored research project, the Field Studies in Urban Desegregated Schools Program, has already reported considerably smoother operation of its ethnographic components (which resemble those of ES) with respect to the fieldwork problems discussed in this paper (see Cassell, 1978: 67). However, the UDS program belongs only marginally in the domain of evaluation research, as conceived by this paper: it did not study a targeted program with a specific allocation of resources, but was instead a more basic research venture aimed at understanding the phenomenon of urban school desegregation.

Outside the education area, other large-scale evaluation research projects aimed at federal demonstration projects are beginning to employ ethnographic components, though with more apparent modification of the conventional ethnographic model. A recent study of a HUD housing allowance program, for example, placed ethnographically trained observers on site for periods of a year to gather data about program agency operations, participating families, and the local community in which the families lived (Chambers, 1977a). The fieldworkers' role definition was more specified than that of the ES counterparts; the product of ethnographic work was not to be an ethnography. Still, fieldworkers' experiences in the HUD study displayed many of the same tensions discussed above. Maintaining rapport and adequate confidentiality were major problems, as was the multiplicity of roles required of fieldworkers.

Addressing Internal Audiences

The ES studies were conceived largely as a summative "experiment." Fieldworkers were supposed to avoid feedback of their findings to those in the program to keep from "contaminating" the experiment, in addition to maintaining adequate confidentiality and objectivity (Colfer, 1976: 36). In so doing, the ES fieldworkers adopted a relatively nonparticipant role, so as to develop an array of qualitative data about change processes for external audiences, who would expect the data to be as "objective" as possible and representative of the "natural" course of events untouched by sophisticated research.

But in many evaluation contexts besides that of the federal demonstration project, the primary audience for evaluation results is the program itself. In these cases, program managers and staff, and sometimes clients, are fed back information about the program's functioning periodically to improve or at least alter its activities. In such cases the sponsor-evaluator-program triangle collapses to a two-sided encounter between evaluator, who is still in some senses external to the program, and evaluatees, who are at once the sponsors and users of evaluative information. This encounter is not unlike the traditional relationship between anthropologist and the community he or she wishes to study, with one important difference: in the formative evaluation situation, the anthropologist is hired *by* the community (or on its behalf) to help it learn about itself.

In this mode of evaluation research, findings generated by the field-worker are typically fed back to program participants in a less digested, less conclusive form than would appear in a written ethnographic account. The result is not "ethnography" in the classical sense of the term, but it is nonetheless in many respects "ethnographic," in that it is exploratory, derived from multiple intensive data sources, reflecting an empathic understanding of participants' experiences and striving for a holistic view of program operations and impacts.

Several brief accounts in the literature suggest the nature of the settings and evaluation contexts in which this approach is useful. In an evaluation of an experimental college unit within a major university, for example, an anthropologist managed to gain the confidence of program participants initially hostile to the idea of evaluation because of prior experience with more conventional evaluations modes (Fitzgerald, 1976). Subsequently, the anthropologist observed program interactions on a continuing basis, periodically relaying his impressions in a form that was acceptable to those conducting the program. Although it is difficult (and perhaps not meaningful) to separate them from the anthropologist's personality, several characteristics of the ethnographic research approach seemed particularly useful in this case: the great emphasis on developing adequate rapport with program participants, the descriptive emphasis of data-collection and interpretation, and the focus of fieldworkers on understanding what the program meant to the participants.

In another case, an ethnographic fieldworker observed students, teachers, and administrators in an urban alternative high school, as part of an evaluation study of the school (Wilson, 1977b). The fieldworker provided regular feedback to those in the program by converting the conventional anthropological analysis "as soon as possible into a form that will help the subjects understand what they are doing to promote or inhibit change" (Wilson, 1977b: 200). The attention paid by the fieldworker to "learning the frameworks by which [program participants] interpret events" appeared to have much to do with the evaluation's capacity to translate findings into terms which were useful for the program.

The fundamental tensions encountered in the ES studies seem less in evidence in these two cases, though it would be hard to argue that the tensions were absent. Other limitations of formative ethnographic work should be noted as well. First, this kind of research approach seems most appropriate in small, fairly manageable systems in which the fieldworker has the capacity to develop ethnographic data *and* at the same time maintain a relationship with the users of the evaluative information. This need only imply that the evaluation be focused on a program within a single institution such as a school or university. Ethnographic work in conjunction with policy formation at the local level has been suggested and is being experimented with, though detailed accounts have yet to be published (Chambers, 1977b). Second, it becomes easier for the fieldworker to lose some of the perspective which a less participant ethnographer might enjoy, and to jump to premature conclusions. Third, there are clear limits on the kinds of information which can be fed back to people within the program. The general problem of maintaining adequate confidentiality exists, although the flow of information is restricted to program participants and does not reach external audiences. Finally, by providing periodic feedback, the fieldworker becomes more of a participant in the situation. New dimensions to the problem of maintaining rapport exist, as the fieldworker becomes identified with certain groups within the program (e.g., Wilson, 1977b: 202). In sum, the fieldworker intrudes more on the program, with subsequent alterations in people's behavior—but that is what formative evaluation intends to do!

Designing More Limited Ethnographic Components

Modest ethnographic components may be included in evaluation research, ones which do not try to generate the approximation of conventional ethnography apparent in the ES studies. Obviously, one can argue whether the spirit of ethnographic research has been lost when one begins to dismember a complex and integrated approach to research so as to accomplish limited evaluation tasks better. This chapter simply presumes that research approaches may be thought of as more or less "ethnographic." The discussion which follows makes no sharp distinction between what is "ethnographic" and much of what is included in discussions of "qualitative approaches to evaluation" (e.g., Clark, 1977; Hamilton et al., 1977).

1. ETHNOGRAPHIC MINI-STUDIES

Short-term fieldwork can be particularly useful for investigating the relationship between variables which program rhetoric or evaluation plan identify as important. One example of this occurred at an early stage of NIE's Experience-Based Career Exploration Program, in which an anthropological "backup study" of student interaction patterns in the EBCE alternative high school program was done by several part-time fieldworkers (Spotts et al., 1974: 171-194). Fieldwork consisted of only 100 observational hours—about a month's time—in which fieldworkers hung around the alternative school building, accompanied students on field trips, and engaged a number of students in conversations about their interaction with each other. The results, summarized in a 23-page ethnographic account, fall far short of rigorous ethnography, but do pinpoint aspects of the program's operation missed by other data-collection instruments.

A concrete illustration from the study demonstrates what this kind of effort can do. The two fieldworkers were able to document a high degree of informal learning-and-teaching going on among students in the EBCE program's learning center. This evidence was taken as supporting the program's assertion that it could create a positive informal learning environment among students. Although the evidence does not stand up to vigorous cross-examination by alternative hypotheses—e.g., the learning pattern would have happened anyway at the regular high school, or the pattern was a temporary reaction of adolescents to a new and different environment—the ethnographic data do document that the pattern did take place, whatever its causes. And the data are considerably *more* convincing in their ethnographic form than they would have been as self-reported rating scale data from a questionnaire, to take but one alternative way of arriving at the finding.

Ethnographic mini-studies such as this can clearly lead to insights into subtle features of program functioning, but the disadvantages of the approach should also be kept in mind. Observations limited to a few students or a small sample of time periods are not necessarily characteristic of most students in the program and most time periods. Short time-frame mini-studies also cannot show change over time particularly well: to do so, extended relationships between fieldworker and program setting would be required. Finally, unless the focus of ethnographic inquiry is central to the thrust of the evaluation, the cost of such mini-studies is difficult to justify.

2. ETHNOGRAPHIC DOCUMENTATION OF PROGRAM IMPLEMENTATION

Although much of what ES fieldworkers did could be thought of as "documenting program implementation," it is clearly possible that a more limited participant observation approach to describing program activities can be invaluable to an evaluation research effort. If the focus of observations is more clearly targeted at the outset, and done with the consent of program personnel, some of the problems of rapport building and confidentiality can be reduced, though they will never be eliminated. The "agency observation" task of the fieldworkers in the HUD housing allowance study mentioned earlier provides one example of this kind of use (see Chambers, 1977a: 259). In that situation, the observer kept a log of twelve specific administrative functions in the agency overseeing the housing allowance program, through regular contact with staff members and through observation of their activities. Daily synopses of these activities were prepared and forwarded to the research firm coordinating the study.

There are some obvious disadvantages of this use of ethnographic fieldwork. The greatest difficulty arises when program personnel and program sponsor develop an adversarial relationship, for whatever reason; in that event, the presence of a fieldworker documenting program activities is likely to generate problems of rapport and confidentiality similar to those reported in the ES case. The discussion of the HUD experiment indicates that there were some difficulties in this regard (Chambers, 1977a: 265).

3. ETHNOGRAPHICALLY-DEVELOPED RESEARCH INSTRUMENTS.

It is also possible to bring the strengths of the ethnographic research approach to bear on the problem of developing sensitive research instruments. A recent account of "ethnographically based" surveys, done as part of a study of drug-related sentiments among Job Corps enrollees, provides an example (Myers, 1977). The survey interview situation was conceptualized as an encounter between cultures as much as a request for information (Myers, 1977: 244-245). Interviewers were hired *prior* to instrument development who were themselves Job Corps members similar to the survey population. Through open-ended interviews and group "rap sessions" with the interviewers, survey designers developed categories of information and items which reflected the nature of social reality as experienced by potential respondents. Item-response categories and wording were also established during these sessions. The instrument development process was simultaneously a process of training and socialization, designed to gain the interviewers' commitment to the purposes and process of research—in a sense, to make the interviewers *themselves* a part of the survey instrument. Emphasis was placed in the training process on the maintenance of rapport between interviewer and interviewee rather than on standardization of item presentation. Data coding formats deliberately sought the interviewers' interpretations of the interview encounter, with special attention paid to their sense of the meanings of nonverbal behavior.

There are, of course, dangers to this kind of approach. Interviewers might have been unsuccessfully socialized to uphold the scientific integrity of the research effort. The approach leaves room for considerable ambiguity in responses, as a result of the unstandardized presentation of items and the interpretive coding process. Furthermore, the technique assumes that the Job Corps enrollees selected as interviewers did not differ systematically from the respondent population; otherwise, important response categories might have been missed in the framing of questions. The technique seems most applicable to relatively homogeneous respondent populations such as that of Job Corps drug users, who were consistently poor minority youth living in urban areas (see Myers, 1977: 251). In such a case, the training and instrument development process was able to tap a common subculture among the interviewer group and at the same time prepare interviewers for a certain type of interview encounter. Finally, one can wonder about the extent to which survey results from this technique are replicable (the published discussion gives no clue).

IN CONCLUSION

This paper has discussed and illustrated several different roles played by ethnography in recent evaluation research, ranging from the approximation of conventional ethnographic research used in the Experimental Schools studies to the modified instrument development process just described.

The experience of those involved in the ES ethnographic work, either at the fieldwork level or that of research coordinator or sponsor, suggests that the conventional ethnographic model of research has considerable difficulty being incorporated intact into the evaluation research process. Fundamental tensions exist, which were especially apparent in the ES case. But the experience with ethnographic fieldwork in the ES studies does indicate that the difficulties are not insurmountable. Detailed ethnographies were created of the change processes at eight of the ten school sites. Case accounts from different sites have begun to be synthesized and interpreted, so as to generate recommendations for further policy action (Herriott, 1979b). The case study data remain as a considerable resource, the potential of which has yet to be tapped. It is too soon to tell how useful the exercise has been, or whether the results or their implications will catch the eye of the many audiences who could make use of them.

Alternative contributions of ethnography to evaluation research exist as well, which reduce some of the basic tensions displayed by the ES case. Each of the alternatives, however, departs more substantially from the conventional ethnographic model than did the ES fieldwork components. In evaluation research addressing internal audiences, the fieldworker's role permits more active participation and analytic procedures are changed to make periodic feedback possible. Reduced "ethnographic" components, such as mini-studies, limited accounts of program implementation, and altered instrument development processes rely on the particular strengths and sensitivities of the ethnographic research mode: its open-endedness, its attention to the meaning system of the group studied, and its focus on subtle interactions between program and surrounding context.

But Who Will Do It?

An important question has been left out of the discussion so far, which provides a suitable note on which to conclude: who can be found with the requisite training, experience, *and* motivation to carry out ethnographic work in future evaluation research efforts? Ethnographic skills have been acquired for the most part through rigorous advanced graduate training in anthropology and qualitative sociology oriented primarily toward academic careers. Under pressure of lack of jobs, ethnographers trained in this way—including many of the ES fieldworkers—have come to contract evaluation research as a "second-best" alternative to grant-supported research in the conventional mode. The tone of complaint is unmistakable in the discussions of the ES experiences. Fieldworkers had to adjust considerably to accommodate complex role relationships and unfamiliar accountability pressures. They had to accept positions as one part—low on the pecking order, at that—of an interdisciplinary research effort, and their resentment of these positions is clear in the titles of articles describing their experiences: "The Anthropologist as Hired Hand" (Clinton, 1975), "The Anthropologist as Go-fer" (Trend, 1976), and "Working for the Man . . ." (Chambers, 1977a).

To the extent that ethnographers have set their sights on academically oriented careers along more conventional anthropological lines, these complaints are justified. Such people will be even less enthusiastic about engaging in the alternative types of ethnographic evaluation actively suggested by this paper. But the expectations of trained ethnographers are changing, and some have pointed toward more central and satisfying roles in evaluation research. One fieldworker advises colleagues to consider nonfieldwork roles in the home office of research firms, synthesizing and interpreting data from quantitative and qualitative sources, designing future research efforts, and managing the work of fieldworkers (Trend, 1976). Another advocates a more active role for fieldworkers in translating their ethnographic findings into action recommendations (Everhart, 1976: 22). Another suggests that ethnographers can perform useful roles as part of "technical assistance" teams, which help program participants act on the information generated by evaluation research (Wilson, 1977b: 200). These and other new roles are being increasingly tried by trained ethnographers with sufficiently positive results to attract others to evaluation research.

Another source of qualified personnel—perhaps a more versatile supply, from the point of view of evaluation research—lies with those who take evaluation research as a primary career goal and focus for graduate training. In training programs which take a broad, interdisciplinary focus, such people can gain a useful working knowledge of ethnographic techniques and skills without necessarily undergoing the anthropologist's full rite of passage (which usually includes a solo fieldwork experience for an extended period of time in a cross-cultural setting). Anthropologists may argue whether fieldworkers without extensive cross-cultural experience have sufficient perspective to think, see, and write competent ethnography (see Wolcott, 1975: 115-116).

But while that debate continues, the evaluation research agenda will not wait. Problems struggle toward solution in the political arena. Evaluation research has much to offer providing it can find the most appropriate and sensitive ways to develop data for each decision situation. The discipline of ethnographic research, too, has much to offer this process, but like any rigorous social science approach, it will lose a good deal of its carefully built disciplinary identity as it enters the fray.

NOTES

1. Though ethnographies tend to interpret social phenomena in functional terms, they need not do so (see Everhart, 1976: 21-22). However, a functional interpretive framework seems typical of much ethnographic work to date.

2. Not all the Project Rural fieldworkers were ethnographers with anthropological credentials; three were sociologists, one an educator (see Herriott, 1977: 109). All had the equivalent of ethnographic training.

3. I am here oversimplifying complex ethical issues which are debated at length within anthropological circles (see Rynkiewich and Spradley, 1976).

REFERENCES

BERREMAN, G. D. (1968) "Ethnography: method and product," in J. A. Clifton (ed.) Introduction to Cultural Anthropology: Essays in the Scope and Methods of the Science of Man. Boston: Houghton Mifflin.

BURNS, A. F. (1976) "On ethnographic process in anthropology and education." Council on Anthropology and Education Quarterly 7, 3.

CARO, F. G. (1971) "Evaluation research: an overview," in F. G. Caro (ed.) Readings in Evaluation Research. New York: Russell Sage.

CASSELL, J. (1978) A Fieldwork Manual for Studying Desegregated Schools. Washington, DC: National Institute for Education.

CHAMBERS, E. (1977a) "Working for the man: the anthropologist in policy relevant research." Human Organization 36, 3.

——— (1977b) "Policy research at the local level." Human Organization 36, 4.

CLARK, W. W., Jr. (1977) "The incorporation of qualitative techniques in educational evaluation." CEDR Quarterly 10, 4.

CLINTON, C. A. (1976) "On bargaining with the devil: contract ethnography and accountability in fieldwork." Council on Anthropology and Education Quarterly 7, 2.

——— (1975) "The anthropologist as hired hand." Human Organization 34, 2.

COLFER, C.J.P. (1976) "Rights, responsibilities, and reports: an ethical dilemma in contract research," in M. Rynkiewich and J. Spradley (eds.) Ethics and Anthropology: Dilemmas in Fieldwork. New York: John Wiley.

CRONBACH, L. J. (1978) Designing Educational Evaluations. Stanford: Stanford University School of Education, Stanford Evaluation Consortium. (preliminary version)

DONNELLY, W. L. (1979) "Arcadia: local initiatives and adaptation," in R. E. Herriott and N. Gross (eds.) The Dynamics of Planned Educational Change. Berkeley: McCutchan.

EVERHART, R. B. (1976) "Ethnography and educational policy: love and marriage or strange bedfellows?" Council on Anthropology and Education Quarterly 7, 3.

——— (1975) "Problems of doing fieldwork in educational evaluation." Human Organization 34, 2.

FILSTEAD, W. J. [ed.] (1970) Qualitative Methodology: Firsthand Involvement in the Social Sciences. Chicago: Markham.

FITZGERALD, T. K. (1976) "The role of the anthropologist in experimental college evaluations: some personal observations," in C. J. Calhoun and F. A. Ianni (eds.) The Anthropological Study of Education. The Hague. Mouton.

FITZSIMMONS, S. J. (1975) "The anthropologist in a strange land." Human Organization 34, 2.

GIDEONSE, H. D. (1979) "Designing federal policies and programs to facilitate local change efforts." in R. E. Herriott and N. Gross (eds.) The Dynamics of Planned Educational Change. Berkeley: McCutchan.

HAMILTON, D., B. McDONALD, C. KING, D. JENKINS, and M. PARLETT [eds.] (1977) Beyond the Numbers Game: A Reader in Educational Evaluation. Berkeley: McCutchan.

HERRIOTT, R. E. (1979a) "The federal context: planning, funding, and monitoring," in R. E. Herriott and N. Gross (eds.) The Dynamics of Planned Educational Change. Berkeley: McCutchan.

—— (1979b) Federal Initiative and Rural School Improvement: Findings from the Experimental School Program. Cambridge, MA: Abt.

—— (1977) "Ethnographic studies in federally-funded multi-disciplinary policy research: some design and implementation issues." Anthropology and Education Quarterly 8, 2.

—— and N. GROSS (1979) The Dynamics of Planned Educational Change. Berkeley: McCutchan.

McCALL, G. J. and J. L. SIMMONS [eds.] (1969) Issues in Participant Observation. Reading, MA: Addison-Wesley.

MESSERSCHMIDT, D. A. (1979) "River District: a search for unity amidst diversity," in R. E. Herriott and N. Gross (eds.) The Dynamics of Planned Educational Change. Berkeley: McCutchan.

MULHAUSER, F. (1975) "Ethnography and policy-making: the case of education." Human Organization 34, 3.

MYERS, V. (1977) "Towards a synthesis of ethnographic and survey methods." Human Organization 36, 3.

PELTO, P. and G. H. PELTO (1978) Anthropological Research: The Structure of Inquiry. Cambridge: Cambridge University Press.

RYNKIEWICH, M. and J. SPRADLEY (1976) Ethics and Anthropology: Dilemmas in Fieldwork. New York: John Wiley.

SPOTTS, R., R. WATKINS, J. EVENSON, and J. BAVRY (1974) Experience-Based Career Education Final Evaluation Report FY 1974, Vol. 2. San Francisco: Far West Laboratory for Educational Research.

TREND, M. G. (1976) "The anthropologist as go-fer." Presented at the annual meeting of the Society for Applied Anthropology. St. Louis, March 17-21.

WAX, R. H. (1971) Doing Fieldwork: Warnings and Advice. Chicago: University of Chicago Press.

WILSON, S. (1977a) "The use of ethnographic techniques in educational research." Review of Educational Research 47, 1.

—— (1977b) "The use of ethnographic methods in educational evaluation." Human Organization 36, 2.

WOLCOTT, H. F. (1975) "Criteria for an ethnographic approach to research in schools." Human Organization 34, 2.

8

Robinson G. Hollister, Jr.
*Mathematica Policy Research
and Swarthmore College*
Peter Kemper
Judith Wooldridge
Mathematica Policy Research

LINKING PROCESS AND IMPACT ANALYSIS
The Case of Supported Work

Most evaluations of employment and training programs fall into two broad types: "impact" analysis, used to assess the program's overall impact on participant outcomes; and "process" analysis, focusing on the internal elements of the program. Impact evaluation asks whether the program is a "success" or "failure" overall, and is typically quantitative in approach. Process analysis, in contrast, asks how the program works with emphasis on identifying ways of improving program operations and design, and is typically qualitative in approach. Although the advantages of combining the two would seem to be obvious, we know of no attempts to link them except in the evaluation currently underway of Supported Work—"a transitional work experience program for certain groups who have traditionally had great difficulty in getting or keeping regular jobs." (Manpower Demonstration and Research Corporation, 1978: 1.) Our paper argues that linking process and impact analysis should be an

---

AUTHORS' NOTE: *The research on which this study is based is part of an evaluation of the Supported Work program for the Manpower Demonstration Research Corporation, whose cooperation the authors appreciate. The MDRC work is being carried out under Employment and Training Administration, U.S. Department of Labor Grant No. 33-36-75-01 and Contract Nos. 30-36-7501 and 30-34-75-02, and Ford Foundation Grant No. 740-0537A. The Employment and Training Association of the Labor Department is the lead agency in a federal funding consortium that sponsors the Supported Work program. The points of view expressed in this paper are those of the authors and do not represent the official position or policies of the sponsoring agencies.*

important objective of evaluation research, and uses a small sample of early data from the Supported Work evaluation to illustrate the potential advantages of linking process with impact analysis. It also argues that the traditional methods of process analysis should be augmented, wherever possible, with the quantitative techniques more usually associated with impact analysis. We wish to emphasize that our objective is to present illustrative material relevant to the methodology of quantitative evaluation research, not to evaluate Supported Work. None of the material presented, therefore, should be taken to represent such an evaluation.[1]

A. USE OF LINKED ANALYSIS TO EVALUATE IMPACTS OF PROGRAM COMPONENTS

A major complaint of program operators, especially those of experimental or demonstration programs, is that the overall impact evaluations have led to summary judgments—most often negative—about programs without an adequate, or fair, assessment of the degree to which specific components (or subprograms) are more or less effective in preparing participants for future employment. Yet, those concerned with questions of whether more or fewer resources should be committed to the program have been quite skeptical of the process analyses that attempt to evaluate these program components because they yield so little information on the overall effects of the program. Moreover, when they do yield evaluative information, it is usually qualitative; and even when it is quantitative, it fails to meet rigorous standards of statistical hypothesis tests. Both program managers and higher level policymakers, then, will be best served by program evaluations that apply the quantitative data and techniques normally associated with impact analysis to process questions about what aspects of the program "work." A few of the specific ways in which such quantitative analysis might improve the management and design of social programs follow.

First, rather than simply accepting or rejecting a central program concept, it may be possible to redesign the structure of the program by eliminating the least effective elements and enhancing the most effective ones. A link between program elements and postprogram impacts is essential to provide information for such an improvement in program design.

Second, in the past, program operators have, of necessity, focused on certain in-program performance measures that they believe are likely to be correlated with postprogram effects, for instance, those on future employment. Attendance, length of time spent in the program, and whether placed in a job at the time of termination are probably the performance indicators most frequently used. There have been, to our knowledge, very few attempts to assess quantitatively the degree to which such in-program performance indicators are correlated with, or predictive of, postprogram outcomes. Using a more quantitative approach to the process variables and combining it with impact data permits an analysis of the usefulness of these performance indicators for feedback to program operators, at least for the particular program for which the link is made and perhaps for generalization to other similar programs.

Third, operators are almost always convinced of the effectiveness of the program they are running. Such conviction is necessary for continued high motivation. They also develop opinions about which aspects of their program are most and least effective. This, too, is essential for effective program management. Linked process and impact data permit the analyst to provide some quantitative tests of the hypothesis which operators develop about "what really matters." In areas other than training and employment, for instance, there are striking examples of strongly held operator opinions about what is effective that have not been supported by quantitative analyses. For example, for decades school teachers and educational experts asserted with complete conviction that academic performance was greatly affected by expenditures per pupil and class size. Numerous quantitative analyses have shown, however, that academic scores are not strongly, if at all, affected by per-pupil expenditure or class size.[2]

Despite these potential benefits, such linked analyses are rare. Several inhibiting factors may explain this failure of evaluation research.

First, there has been a lack of data. Data on program outcomes—especially long-term follow-up on postprogram employment experience—is expensive to collect and, thus, not often available. Even when it is available, data on the program experience of the same individuals suitable for quantitative analysis seldom exist. The combination of both types of data and the capacity to link them is rare indeed.

Second, availability of data is not enough. There must be large enough samples of participants exposed to *particular* program elements to assure that an effect of reasonable size will be statistically detectable. When there are several program elements to be evaluated, these sample size requirements may become prohibitively large.

Third, since assignment of participants to different program elements is not normally subject to a carefully controlled and documented process, results that appear to be treatment effects may be due to selection bias. Do operators assign their best workers to their favorite treatment (sometimes referred to as "creaming"), or do they assign the worst, those in most need, to the treatment they consider most powerful? Or do the participants themselves tend to volunteer for or seek out program experiences which somehow fit their personal "style"? If either is the case, then differentials in postprogram impacts will result, not from differences in program treatments but from differences in the types of individuals who are assigned to (or select themselves for) those treatments. To the extent that the factors causing operators to select particular types of individuals for particular treatments are measurable and data on them available to the evaluator, statistical methods can correct for the selection process in order to yield unbiased estimates of treatment effects. The same is true if participant self-selection is determined by such measured characteristics. However, where selection by the operator or by the participants involves unmeasured characteristics, the estimated treatment effects may be subject to such selection bias.

The Supported Work evaluation is large enough, and the data collection strategies rigorous enough to allow the necessary kinds of data to be collected for an evaluation of the postprogram effects of different in-program factors. As already mentioned, the overall evaluation is not yet completed. The next sections, however, illustrate—for a small subsample of early observations—the potential of the linked approach.

B. SUPPORTED WORK AND ITS DATA BASE

Supported Work is a transitional work experience program directed toward four groups of people who have traditionally had great difficulty in getting or keeping regular jobs: ex-offenders who have recently been released from prison or jail; ex-addicts currently in treatment; young school dropouts, many of whom have delinquent histories; and women who are longtime recipients of welfare payments under the Aid to Families with Dependent Children (AFDC) program. Supported Work offers such people a job and the opportunity to make good in it, and a chance to gain permanent employment in the regular labor market. . . .

Supported Work was launched on a national level in March, 1975, in an effort to test the effectiveness of a program which had shown substantial promise on the local level in New York City. In the first phase, 13 sites participated. By the end of the second full year of the demonstration, in June, 1977, two more sites had been added and over 5,400 people had enrolled in the program.

The demonstration is sponsored by a consortium of five federal agencies, led by the Employment and Training Administration of the U.S. Department of Labor, and the Ford Foundation's Division of National Affairs. it is managed by the Manpower Demonstration Research Corporation, a nonprofit organization which was established to design and supervise large-scale demonstration and research projects. Resources for the demonstration come from a combination of direct grants from the national sponsors, federal revenue-sharing type funds raised by the local programs, and revenues generated through the sale of goods and services produced by supported workers.

The demonstration includes a comprehensive research component, which seeks to answer whether supported work results in improved earnings and employment and reduced criminal activity, drug use, and reliance on welfare. The research contractors for Supported Work are Mathematica Policy Research, Inc., Princeton, New Jersey, and the Institute for Research on Poverty of the University of Wisconsin at Madison [MDRC, 1978: 1-2].

At ten of the fifteen Supported Work sites, eligible applicants for the program were assigned randomly to an experimental group or to a control group. Those assigned to the experimental group were given the opportunity to participate in Supported Work. Periodic interviews were administered immediately before this random assignment and then again nine and eighteen months later. The interviews contain basic demographic and postprogram data, as well as data on other outcomes of interest (e.g., welfare dependence and criminal activity). Data used in this chapter are limited to postprogram earnings data for an early sample of 1,033 individuals.

Even more important to our ability to do a quantitative process analsysis than the postprogram outcome data is a carefully designed and controlled Management Information System (MIS). The MIS comprises operational forms submitted regularly and periodically from the various program sites, and contains a wealth of information on the characteristics of the work projects and supervisors, as well as information on the characteristics and in-program performance of the participants. Seven forms are included in the MIS. Table 1 presents a summary of these forms, including their contents, the frequency of submission, and the person responsible for their completion.

The components of the MIS provide an extremely rich data base for the analysis of the effect of different program experiences of Supported Work participants. Although the richness of the data base makes it complex (since the various components of the MIS data are large in volume and submitted at varying time intervals), its data elements can be integrated into a single observation for each program participant, providing quantitative summaries of his or her program experience.[3] The quantitative summaries have been merged with the outcome data obtained from participant interviews, thus linking the MIS data on process with the interview data on program impact to provide a powerful analysis capability.

In summary, the data base contains program experience data on

- project characteristics
- supervisor characteristics

Table 1: Summary of MIS Forms

Form	Data	Frequency	Who Fills in Form
Enrollment	Target group, family structure, income sources, race, education, employment history, skills and training, previous convictions, previous treatment for drug or alcohol use, probation.	Once—completed upon intake into program.	Program intake officers fill out form by recording responses of Supported Workers to questions.
Time Sheet	Hours spent on projects, ancillary services, sick, holiday, vacation, suspension, inactivation, and other; also includes days present, minutes late or left early; bonus indicator and evaluation code.	Weekly.	Payroll clerks. Some information is transcribed from weekly time card which is filled out by crew chiefs.
Status Change	Indicates initial start date, promotion, demotion, inactivation, reactivation, suspension, transfer to new crew; termination; also includes reasons for various status changes.	When appropriate.	Appropriate program staff member.
Crew Supervision Assignment	Identifies relationship between supervisor and crew.	When appropriate.	Operations staff.
Project Summary	Type of customer, competitive bid or not, type of supervision, occupation and industry DOT and SIC codes, type of job; type of reimbursement (if any) for project.	When a project starts.	Operations staff.
Supervisor Profile	Information on supervisor, including education, age, race, supervisory experience, skills training, attitudes to Supported Work supervision.	Once–after two-months supervisory experience.	Supervisors.

- crew characteristics
- supportive services
- the site and its age.

For outcomes, the following measures are available:

- attendance
- type of termination and length of stay in the program
- post-program employment status and earnings
- other outcome measures.

Finally, the data base includes information on:

- individual characteristics
- local labor market conditions.[4]

This data base can be used to analyze a wide variety of questions. To illustrate the type of analysis possible, we have used some very preliminary results based on an early sample of participants to answer, on the basis of a single outcome measure—non-Supported-Work earnings during the eighteenth month after enrollment—two questions. First, how well does the time and type of termination (a success indicator available to program operators) predict postprogram earnings? And second, how are post-program earnings related to participant experience during the program— the type of work project, characteristics of supervisors, crew characteristics, and supportive services?

C. TERMINATION AS AN INDICATOR OF POSTPROGRAM SUCCESS

As noted above, one way of improving the management of social programs is to provide managers with feedback on performance. Yet, participant follow-up data is costly to collect, and feedback from it is subject to a long time lag. Routine feedback to managers of employment and training programs is presently limited to short-term indicators, such as attendance, and intermediate-term indicators, such as length of stay and whether or not the reason for termination was to take a regular job. Management decisions must be based on these short- and intermediate-term indicators under the assumption that they predict postprogram performance. We test that assumption in this section, by examining the relation between postprogram earnings and the type and time of termination.

Table 2 presents the results of regressions of non-Supported-Work earnings during the eighteenth month after enrollment on the reason for termination from the program and two sets of control variables. Both experimental and control group observations have been included in these regressions to enable us tö separate the effect on earnings of the reason for termination from the effect of other factors that also affect earnings.

Reasons for termination have been grouped into three categories—positive, negative, and neutral. Dummy variables for the different Supported Work sites are included to control for labor market differences across cities. The results show rather large and statistically significant differences by type of termination. Experimentals who terminate for positive reasons have eighteen-month earnings $237 higher than the average for controls, whereas those terminating for negative reasons have earnings $50 below controls. (Earnings of those terminating for neutral reasons were not significantly different from controls.) Overall average earnings during the eighteenth month for this preliminary sample was $148. The magnitude, relative to this mean, of the difference in earnings by type of termination thus suggests that type of termination is a good predictor of postprogram earnings, at least as measured eighteen months after enrollment. When we say "good predictor of postprogram earnings," we refer to the fact that the mean value of earnings for positive terminees is substantially (and statistically significantly) higher than the mean for the sample as a whole. However, it should be noted that the overall regression accounts for only a small percentage of the variance in eighteenth-month earnings (R^2 adjusted = .09) so that *any* "predictor" of eighteenth-month earnings taken from the measured characteristics represented in the regression is relatively weak.

It is not clear from these results, however, whether the earnings differences are due to differences among individuals that were present at the start of the program—differences which influenced both type of termination and postprogram earnings. Column 2 of Table 2 shows the effect on the regression results of including several measured characteristics of experimentals and controls at time of random assignment.[5] (Here, again, including the control group observations improves the capacity to separate the effect of termination type from that of individual differences.) That the results change only slightly suggests that the observed differences in postprogram earnings by type of termination are not due to differences in the *measured* characteristics of individuals included in the regression. They may, of course, be due to differences in unmeasured characteristics. The issue of such selection bias is discussed further in Section E below.

Program managers have information not only on the type of termination but also on the length of stay in the program, and retention of participants in a program is frequently viewed as an important measure of program

Table 2: Type of Termination as a Predictor of Postprogram Earnings

Variable	Independent Variables Included in the Regressions	
	Termination Type and Site	Termination Type, Site, and Individual Characteristics
Termination Type[a]		
Positive	237***	208***
Negative	−50**	−46*
Neutral	5	30
Site		
Atlanta	102*	95
Chicago	86**	86**
Hartford	19	35
Jersey City	45	68**
Newark	9	−10
Oakland	88**	38
Philadelphia (omitted)	− −	− −
San Francisco	107***	43
Individual Characteristics		
Ethnic Group		
White	− −	93**
Spanish	− −	− −
Black (omitted)	− −	− −
Age (Nonyouth Target Groups)[b]		
Less than 25 years	− −	−21
26-30 years (omitted)	− −	− −
More than 30 years	− −	−3
Female (Non-AFDC Target Groups)[c]	− −	−77**
Number of Dependents	− −	4
Education		
High school diploma	− −	66**
Has had job training	− −	−32
Employment Experience		
Has held a full time job	− −	19
Earnings last year (000)	− −	6
Target Group		
AFDC[c]	− −	−19
Ex-addict	− −	−45
Ex-offender	− −	− −
Youth[b]	− −	−64
Individual is a crew chief	− −	187***
Statistics		
Adjusted R[2]	.05	.09
F-statistic	6.20	5.04
Number of Observations	1,033	1,033

success in itself. Table 3 presents estimates of the effect of length of stay on postprogram earnings. The length of stay is divided into four discrete time periods for each type of termination. For simplicity of presentation, we report only the coefficients of the time and type of termination variables, omitting individual characteristics and site variables from the table, although these variables were included in the regression from which the coefficients displayed in Table 3 are drawn.

Not surprisingly, the pattern of coefficients with these disaggregated categories of termination type conform roughly to the average effect by termination type reported in Table 2—in general, positive terminations have a positive effect on postprogram employment and negative terminations have a negative effect. However, the disaggregation by the number of weeks at which the termination occurred provides some interesting qualifications to this result. First, the relationship between positive terminations and postprogram earnings does not become significantly positive unless the termination occurs after the eighth week; positive termination in the first eight weeks bears no significant relationship to postprogram earnings. Second, the relation between positive termination and earnings reaches a peak when the termination occurs between the twenty-seventh and thirty-ninth week, declining thereafter. Third, negative terminations show a negative relationship with earnings that is small in magnitude and insignificant until the twenty-seventh week.

Finally, although neutral terminations overall were not significantly related to postprogram earnings, Table 3 shows that the overall result masks a difference in effect depending on the time of termination. The relation between postprogram earnings and neutral termination is negative but insignificant during the first 39 weeks. For neutral terminations that

---

Notes to Table 2:

 *Statistically significant at the 90% level using a two-tailed test.
 **Statistically significant at the 95% level using a two-tailed test.
***Statistically significant at the 99% level using a two-tailed test.

a. Type of termination categories are defined as follows:

 Positive Termination: The participant left in order to take a job or to go to school during the study period.

 Negative Termination: The participant was fired, incarcerated, or left because of dissatisfaction with the program during the study period.

 Neutral Termination: The participant left during the study period because of sickness, to look after the family, because there was no work available in the program, or because forced to graduate.

b. The age variables cover only the target groups other than youth (who are all 21 years old or younger). Thus, the youth variables combine the effect of age and target group status.

c. The female variable covers only the target groups other than AFDC (who are all female). Thus the AFDC variable combines the effect of being female and in that target group.

Table 3: Type and Time of Termination as
Predictor of Postprogram Earnings

Type and Time of Termination[a]	Independent Variables Included	
	Termination Type and Site	Termination Type, Site, and Individual Characteristics
Positive		
Weeks 1-8	36	50
Weeks 9-26	192***	153**
Weeks 27-39	377***	337***
Weeks 40-52	281***	253***
Negative		
Weeks 1-8	−39	−27
Weeks 9-26	−16	−7
Weeks 27-39	−110**	−110**
Weeks 40-52	−85*	−101**
Neutral		
Weeks 1-8	6	15
Weeks 9-26	−89	−57
Weeks 27-39	−77	−37
Weeks 40-52	284***	283***
Statistics		
Adjusted R-squared	.06	.09
F-statistic	4.37	4.26
Number of Observations	1,033	1,033

NOTE: In addition to the variables shown, these regressions also included the individual characteristics shown in Table 2. Since they are included primarily as control variables, they are not reported here.

*Statistically significant at the 90% level using a two-tailed test.
**Statistically significant at the 95% level using a two-tailed test.
***Statistically significant at the 99% level using a two-tailed test.

a. Type of termination categories are defined as follows:

Positive Termination: The participant left in order to take a job or to go to school during the study period.

Negative Termination: The participant was fired, incarcerated, or left because of dissatisfaction with the program during the study period.

Neutral Termination: The participant left during the study period because of sickness, to look after the family, because there was no work available in the program, or because forced to graduate.

occur between the fortieth and fifty-second weeks, in contrast, the relationship to postprogram earnings is positive and statistically significant. Since forced graduations are included in the neutral category, these results suggest that for participants who stay in the program a long time, pressure to take a regular job may be an effective policy. (The decline from the 27-39 week period to the 40-52 week period in the effect of positive terminations also appears consistent with this hypothesis.) Although this evidence is suggestive, further work examining follow-up earnings in subsequent time periods and disaggregating the neutral termination category into forced graduations and others would be necessary to address this question more definitively.

The results presented here illustrate one type of analysis that could be performed with linked process and impact data. As we have noted, the results may be affected by selection biases that result from factors not measured by the control variables included in the regression and must therefore be regarded as preliminary. Nonetheless, they suggest that one type of performance indicator often used by program operators,[6] namely type of termination and length of stay, may be significantly related to postprogram performance at least for this particular program. They also provide some hints as to policy regarding how long participants should be encouraged or allowed to stay in the program.

D. DURING-PROGRAM EXPERIENCE AND POST-PROGRAM EARNINGS

Another type of analysis that is potentially of even more policy use than the one illustrated in the previous section is examination of the relation between variations in the program treatment and postprogram outcomes. Table 4 provides this type of information. The results reported are for a regression of postprogram earnings on variables measuring the variation in program experience—characteristics of the project participants worked on, their immediate work supervisor, their work peers, and the supportive services they received. Several of the coefficients are statistically significant and large in magnitude:

- The type of work project appears to be related to postprogram earnings, with retailing and furniture-repair projects having negative coefficients and social service and auto-repair projects having positive ones.

- The type of supervisor may also affect outcomes. Supervisors with more education are associated with lower postprogram earnings of participants. Previous experience working with the Supported Work target groups is positively related to postprogram earnings, although other types of experience are not. The supervisors' strictness (according to their own reports) is significantly related to earnings, with stricter supervisors being associated with lower earnings. In addition, if a work crew has a participant crew chief (in addition to a regular staff supervisor), the project is associated with higher postprogram earnings.

- The number of times an individual changes crews is positively associated with postprogram earnings, a somewhat surprising result. Crew characteristics

Table 4: Regression of Postprogram Earnings on Program Experience (Controlling for Individual Characteristics)

Variable	Regression Coefficient
Industry of Work Project	
Grounds Maintenance	−6
Painting	15
Construction	− −
Manufacturing	−82
Retailing	−202***
Clerical Services	87
Building Maintenance Services	−2
Other Services to Business	27
Auto Repair Services	222**
Furniture Repair Services	−377**
Social Services	336***
Type of Supervision	
By program	−68
By crew chief	70**
Supervisor's Age and Education	
Age	−3
Highest grade completed	−17*
Has a license or training certificate	59
Supervisor's Prior Experience	
Worked with target groups	125**
Counseled	−40
Supervised	27
Military supervisory experience	52
Same type of work	−68
Trained	−48
Supervisor's Similarity to Participant	
Sex	34
Race	−26
Convictions	−60
Drug treatment	19
Supervisor's Style	
Primary objective getting job done	81
Strictness	−57***
Businesslike toward participants	67
Crew Size	
1 to 3 (omitted)	− −
4 to 7	59
8 to 10	86
Over 10	57

Table 4 (Continued)

Variable	Regression Coefficient
Characteristics of Other Crew Members	
Proportion worked full time	−203*
Average highest grade completed	−3
Average age	5
Number of Crew Changes (per week)	169***
Supportive Services	
Counselling	73
Job search training	73**
Job skills training	−32*
Classroom education	54
Second year of program operation	
Adjusted R^2	.10
F-statistic	2.80
Number of Observations	1,033

NOTE: Also included in the regression, but not reported, were individual characteristics and dummy variables for each site and target group, which are the same as those reported in Table 2.

*Statistically significant at the 90% level using a two-tailed test.

**Statistically significant at the 95% level using a two-tailed test.

***Statistically significant at the 99% level using a two-tailed test.

are, however, generally insignificant (although if other members of the crew worked full time before Supported Work, postprogram earnings are lower—the opposite of the peer group effect one might have expected).

● The extent of the supportive services provided is an important aspect of program design. The regression shows a positive association between postprogram earnings and job search training[7] and a negative association with job skills training.

We have refrained here from extensive discussion, explanation or hypothesezing about the meaning of the statistical significance or insignificance of particular program experience variables. There are several reasons for this restraint. The sample used is small and preliminary. We have not done sufficient investigation of this sample to feel confident that particular apparently significant results might not arise from collinearities in the data (though it is highly unlikely that all significant coefficients are due to such problems). And the results remain potentially subject to selection bias due to unmeasured characteristics.

Most important, we feel that such quantitative results are illustrative of only a first step in the sequence that would make up an ideal process analysis. The results serve to illustrate how suggestions for further inquiry about program process might be initiated. (For example, the persistent positive effects of job search training should lead to a more careful gathering of detailed information about what sort of job search assistance was provided, at what stage, and to whom.) They also may yield some indications, which program operators could attempt to test in subsequent periods, of directions for improvement in program design. (These might include changes in project mix, increased use of participant crew chiefs, hiring of supervisors who have had experience with the target group and do not characterize themselves as "strict.") Equally valuable, these results might serve to discourage investment of resources in changes which appear unlikely to be effective (e.g., keeping crew sizes small).

The further inquiry and reaction to such an initial quantitative analysis should lead to a sequence of interactions between the analysts and the program operators that could refine the analysis and the programs.[8]

E. SELECTION BIAS

In the preceding sections, we have stated repeated reservations about particular results because they may be affected by selection bias. Before drawing conclusions, therefore, we need to discuss this issue a bit more fully.

There has been considerable controversy in the evaluation literature over the issue of selection bias in data generated by any process other than an experiment with random assignment of subjects to treatments. We do not wish to get deeply embroiled in that controversy here, but rather limit ourselves to a few comments relevant to the sorts of data we have described.

It has already been demonstrated that to the extent that selection is explicit and information is gathered about the explicit selection process, quantitative methods permit unbiased estimation of program effects even where the assignment process in not random (Cain, 1975). This suggests that better efforts at documenting selection processes should be made in order to enhance the interpretability of the program data.

There remains, however, the problem of unrecorded selection on unmeasured characteristics, either on the part of an administrator who assigns participants or through self-selection on the part of participants themselves. Here, there are two different general paths which might be followed. First, one might seek improved methodology for removing or reducing selection biases from a given set of data that has already been gathered. Second, one can seek to set up a sequential process of data gathering and program alteration which would reduce the effects of selection bias. Let us discuss each of these paths briefly.

With regard to improved methodology, this issue of selection bias in quantitative analysis in social science in general, as well as evaluation in particular, has recently received increased attention. Formal statistical techniques for estimating the degree of selection and removing selection bias have been developed by Heckman (1976) and Maddala and Lee (1976), and their adaptation to evaluation research has been suggested by Barnow, Cain, and Goldberger (1978). (We have initiated some attempts to use these techniques for reestimating the termination results reported in Section C above. These techniques are appropriate for dichotomous or polychotomous treatments, however, and at present it is not clear how to extend these methods to situations in which the treatment is highly multidimensional, as, for example, with the large set of program experience variables represented in Section D above.) Another methodological approach with which we have been experimenting uses early performance measures—in our cases, attendance—to obtain proxies for unmeasured characteristics, and uses these as additional control variables in regressions like those used in Sections C and D (Hollister et al., 1978). The theoretical basis for this approach, however, is not as yet well developed.

The second path to reduction in potential selection bias is through a sequential interaction between analysts and program operators. As already indicated at the close of Section D, results of the sort reported in Sections C and D should be regarded as the first step in such a process. Results from this first stage should be fed back to program operators. Discussions of the results can lead either to reformulation of the variables in the analysis or to adjustments in program processes. A second data gathering and testing of results could follow. Where there is a particularly controversial finding, it may be possible to convince operators to test the proposition by random assignment among the treatments in question, at least for a period of time.

Although selection bias is a potential problem, it is important to keep perspective on this issue and not to forego analysis which can be useful even when the degree of bias is uncertain.

F. CONCLUSION

It is our belief that linking process and impact analysis should be an important objective of evaluation research. The results presented here link the types of analysis in an important but limited way. Process data on program experience have been quantified and linked with outcome data, and a "quantitative process analysis" has been performed. But, as we have suggested above, this is just the first step in what we have sketched out as an ideal sequence of interaction between analysis and program operators.

Our own experience to date with attempts to proceed further with this ideal sequential analysis leaves us with few illusions about the ease with which it can be accomplished in practice. We have gathered general qualitative impressions from program operators about the process of selection and assignment of participants to treatments. A few of the program managers' perceptions about important program features have been quantified and "tested" (e.g., the effects of crew size and racial similarity of supervisors and participants). But it has proved difficult to push the interaction much beyond this initial stage.

The empirical requirements for realization of the ideal are, obviously, prodigious. We list just a few. The program must be of sufficient scale and duration to yield samples large enough to carry out statistical hypothesis tests of adequate power. (We have in fact been surprised that we have been able to obtain significant results with a sample of a little over 1,000.) There must be an internal data system, with standardized forms and reasonable quality control, which reports regular individualized data. Data must be processed rapidly and converted into analytical files so that analysis can be completed and fed back to program operators in a relatively short period.[9] Data from the postprogram interviews must be processed and merged with the program data. Fast feedback is likely to enhance data quality as operators see the fruits of their data input efforts. Analysts must develop an ability to explain basic aspects of their data analysis to program operators. They must also increase their sensitivity to forms of analysis which would be most useful for the month-to-month operating of the program (as contrasted with more fundamental program redesign). Finally, operators must be convinced that this type of analysis can be used not simply to pass negative judgments on their performance but to help them enhance performance.

Above all, such an interaction implies a view of quantitative process analysis that differs from that of many quantitative analysts. Results should, in our judgment, be viewed not as tests of formal models of behavior or as causal relationships but rather as descriptive of what happened. Process research is undertaken in an effort to understand how the program works. Such an effort, even when quantitative in methodology is necessarily an exploratory and inductive process. The statistical results are most useful, therefore, if they are viewed as descriptive and interpreted in light of practical understanding of how the program operates, including qualitative assessments of the effectiveness of different program experiences. Any conclusions based on such an interpretation are necessarily tentative and judgmental. But they are less so than conclusions based solely on anecdotes and hunches without grounding in objective outcome measures. What we are suggesting, then, is not the substitution of statistical analysis for practical understanding of the program but the interaction of quantitative analysts, qualitative process analysts, and program managers in a sequential search for ways of improving the program's design and implementation.

Linking process and impact analysis should not be oversold. We have tried to present a balanced though brief review of potential benefits as well as potential pitfalls and difficulties. Participants' responses to program experiences are complex; and potential for data biases, serious. Yet, improved management and design of public programs pose an important challenge for those concerned about social policy. We believe linking process and impact analysis can help in that effort.

NOTES

1. Readers primarily interested in Supported Work and its evaluation should consult the several reports directed specifically at its overall impact. Information on the status and availability of these reports, as well as other publications concerning Supported Work, can be obtained from the Manpower Demonstration Research Corporation, 3 Park Avenue, New York, New York 10016.

2. The findings of these studies have not all been negative, however. As Hanushek (forthcoming), in his useful review of such studies, notes, the studies do provide "conclusive evidence that differences among schools and teachers are important in achievement. . . . Yet, the identification and measurement of *specific* teacher or school attributes which are important is much less certain" (emphasis added).

3. For a complete discussion of the MIS data and its manipulation for research purposes, see Hollister et al. (1978).

4. These have been obtained from published data sources.

5. Although not of primary interest for this analysis, it is worth noting that the coefficients of the individual characteristics included in the regressions in Column 2 are statistically significant and generally consistent with other research on the factors that affect earnings. Blacks earn less than whites and Spanish-speaking individuals. Women earn less than men. Earnings are higher for those who hold a diploma. These characteristics could also be interacted with experimental status to determine whether the program is more or less effective with particular subgroups of participants. Such an analysis might yield policy recommendations for targeting the program at particular subgroups of the client population currently served. Further, by interacting individual characteristics with program variants or subprograms, it may be possible to suggest ways of improving the assignment of participants to within-program variations in experience. This research lies beyond the illustrative purposes of this paper.

6. Attendance is another performance indicator which program operators (and employers) often use. We have carried out similar analyses of the relationship of this indicator to postprogram earnings. However, because of limitations of space, we do not report the details of this analysis. It did show that attendance rates are significantly related to postprogram earnings.

7. One might expect this to be a spurious correlation—those who stay in the program long enough to get job search training are also more likely to get a job (even if they had not received the training). In regressions, not reported here, the type and time of termination were added to the equation but the coefficient of job search training remained significant and about the same size. This suggests that the correlation may not be spurious.

8. In the Supported Work Demonstration the purely quantitative research evaluation was supplemented with a more qualitative evaluation. Part of the inquiry which followed the first stage process analysis involved and was worked out through the staff carrying out the qualitative analysis. For a description of that analysis see Ball (1977).

9. Probably the chief reason for our failure to push the interactions with program operators further was that we were unable to provide this rapid feedback. We believe our failure in this regard was due to the fact we were creating procedures not attempted before, but it may be that any such large-scale effort will bog down, even when the course is better charted in advance. Lags in obtaining follow-up data from participant interviews, however, make rapid feedback based on follow-up data impossible.

REFERENCES

BALL, J. (1977) Implementing Supported Work: Job Creation Strategies During the First Year of the National Demonstration. New York: Manpower Research and Demonstration.

BARNOW, B., G. CAIN, and A. GOLDBERGER (1978) "Issues in the analysis of selection bias." University of Wisconsin Department of Economics. Presented at the American Economics Association meeting, August.

CAIN, G. (1975) "Regression and selection models to improve non-experimental comparisons," in C. A. Bennett and A. A. Lumsdaine (eds.) Evaluation and Experiment. New York: Academic Press.

HANUSHEK, E. (forthcoming) "Conceptual and empirical issues in the estimation of educational production functions." Journal of Human Resources.

HECKMAN, J. (1976) "The common structure of statistical models of truncation, sample selection and limited dependent variables and a sample estimator of such models." Annals of Economic and Social Measurement 5: 475-492.

HOLLISTER, R., P. KEMPER, V. LEACH, and J. WOOLDRIDGE (1978) Analysis of the Determinants of Attendance and Termination Rates in the Supported Work Demonstration. Draft report submitted to the Manpower Demonstration and Research Corporation by Mathematica Policy Research, Princeton, June.

MADDALA, G. S. and L.-F. LEE (1976) "Recursive models with qualitative endogenous variables." Annals of Economic and Social Measurement 5: 525-545.

Manpower Demonstration and Research Corporation (1978) Summary of the Second Annual Report on the National Supported Work Demonstration. August. New York: MDRC.

ABOUT THE CONTRIBUTORS

HOWARD S. BECKER is Professor of Sociology at Northwestern University and author of *Outsiders* and *Sociological Work*. He has written on research methods and on photography, and has taught photography at the Visual Studies Workshop and the San Francisco Art Institute.

DONALD T. CAMPBELL received his Ph.D. in Psychology from the University of California at Berkeley in 1947 and has taught at Northwestern University for the last 25 years. He is a past president of the American Psychological Association and a member of the National Academy of Sciences. He has received the Distinguished Scientific Contribution Award of the American Psychological Association, the Kurt Lewin Memorial Award of the Society for the Psychological Study of Social Issues, and the first Myrdal Prize in Science from the Evaluation Research Society in 1977. Currently, he is Albert Schweitzer Professor in the Maxwell School at Syracuse University.

THOMAS D. COOK is Professor of Psychology at Northwestern University, where he is also Director of the Social Psychology Training Program. He has coauthored *Sesame Street Revisited, Quasi-Experimentation: Design and Analysis Issues for Field Settings,* and *Criminal Victimization of the Elderly*. He has also edited, with assistance, the third volume of the *Evaluation Studies Review Annual,* and he is on the editorial board of *Evaluation Quarterly, Evaluation Magazine, Knowledge: Creation, Dissemination, and Utilization.*

WILLIAM J. FILSTEAD is Associate Professor of Psychiatry and Behavioral Sciences at Northwestern University, where he is coordinator of evaluation research for both the Institute of Psychiatry and the Northwestern Community Mental Health Center. He received his Ph.D. in sociology from Northwestern University in 1973. He began his career at Lutheran General Hospital's Alcoholism Treatment Center in 1969, where he was primarily responsible for research and program evaluation activities. His areas of interest are in clinical management information systems, qualitative methods and evaluation, and applied research in alcoholism. Dr. Filstead is the author of numerous articles and books, among which are *Qualitative Methodology; Introduction to Deviance,* with Jean Rossi; *The Therapeutic Community,* with Jean Rossi and Mark Keller; *Alcohol Problems: New Thinking and New Directions;* and, with John Mayer, *Adolescence and Alcohol.*

ROBINSON G. HOLLISTER, Jr., is a senior fellow at Mathematica Policy Research and Professor of Economics at Swarthmore College. Mr. Hollister is currently principal investigator of the Supported Work project. He played a leading role in the New Jersey Negative Income Tax Experiment and is an internationally recognized expert on poverty and income maintenance program evaluation.

FRANCIS A.J. IANNI is Professor and Director of the Horace Mann-Lincoln Institute, Teachers College Columbia University and Consultant in Medical Psychology at St. Luke Hospital Psychiatry Center. Before coming to Columbia, he was Associate Commissioner for Research, U.S. Office of Education, and he has taught at Yale University and University College Addis Ababa, Ethiopia. He received his Ph.D. in Anthropology from Pennsylvania State University and is a graduate of the New York Psychoanalytic Institute.

PETER KEMPER is an economist at Mathematica Policy Research. His research has included studies of the efficiency of local government police and refuse collection services and of the intrametropolitan location decisions of manufacturing firms. He is currently participating in the evaluation of the national Supported Work demonstration, with special interest in benefit-cost and process analysis. Before joining MPR, Mr. Kemper was Assistant Professor of Economics at Swarthmore College.

MICHAEL S. KNAPP is currently a Ph.D. candidate in the Sociology of Education Program at the Stanford University School of Education. He has been an active member of the Stanford Evaluation Consortium for the past two years, and is also a trainee in the NIMH-sponsored Organizations and Mental Health Research Training Program operated by a consortium of faculty from the Stanford University Sociology Department, Business School, and School of Education. His particular interests include the organizational dimensions of evaluative research, the application of alternative methodologies to the problems of evaluation design, and the synthesis of qualitative and quantitative approaches to evaluation.

MARGARET TERRY ORR is currently a research associate at the Horace Mann-Lincoln Institute, Teachers College, Columbia University, where she supervises several state and local research and evaluation projects in the field of education. She is an adjunct assistant professor in the Department of Educational Administration.

CHARLES S. REICHARDT is Assistant Professor of Psychology at the University of Denver. He did his graduate work in the Evaluation and Methodology Program in the Department of Psychology at Northwestern University. His articles have appeared in such journals as *Evaluation Quarterly, Evaluation Magazine,* and *Journal of Educational Statistics,* and he authored a chapter on the statistical analysis of data from nonequivalent groups in *Quasi-Experimentation,* by Cook and Campbell. He has also served as a consultant for many research companies and researchers at several universities.

M. G. TREND is a senior analyst for Abt Associates Inc., a contract research firm in Cambridge, Massachusetts. Currently, he is deputy director of the Minnesota Work Equity Research Project, a welfare reform demonstration. In the past, he has worked on research projects in housing, legal services delivery, rural education, and day care. A social anthropologist by training, Dr. Trend is associate editor for *Human Organization,* the journal for the Society for Applied Anthropology. He is also a contributing editor for *Practicing Anthropology,* a practitioner-oriented journal for nonacademic anthropologists.

JUDITH WOOLDRIDGE is a researcher at Mathematica Policy Research who has worked principally on health and manpower projects at MPR, including the Physician Capacity Utilization Surveys and the Supported Work Demonstration Evaluation. She is currently researcher and project manager for the Evaluation of Health Manpower Shortage Areas and is acting director of research support. Before joining MPR, Ms. Wooldridge was a research associate at the Centre for Urban and Regional Studies, University of Birmingham, United Kingdom.